WITNESS FROM BEYOND

New cosmic concepts on
death and survival
received from the late
A. D. MATTSON, S.T.D.,
through the clairvoyant,
Margaret Flavell Tweddell

transcribed and edited by
Ruth Mattson Taylor

HAWTHORN BOOKS, INC.
Publishers/NEW YORK

WITNESS FROM BEYOND

Copyright © 1975, by Ruth Mattson Taylor. Copyright under International and Pan-American Copyright Conventions. All rights reserved, including the right to reproduce this book or portions thereof in any form, except for the inclusion of brief quotations in a review. All inquiries should be addressed to Hawthorn Books, Inc., 260 Madison Avenue, New York, New York 10016. This book was manufactured in the United States of America and published simultaneously in Canada by Prentice-Hall of Canada, Limited, 1870 Birchmount Road, Scarborough, Ontario.

Library of Congress Catalog Card Number: 75-5033

ISBN: 0-8015-8776-X

1 2 3 4 5 6 7 8 9 10

To the Invisible Communion of Saints
from whom this book is received

That which was from the beginning,
which we have heard, which we have
seen with our eyes, which we have
looked upon and touched with our
hands, concerning the word of life—
the life was made manifest,
and we saw it, and testify to it,
and proclaim to you the eternal life
which was with the Father and was
made manifest to us—
that which we have seen and heard
we proclaim also to you, so that
you may have fellowship with us;
and our fellowship is with the Father
and with his Son Jesus Christ.
And we are writing this that your
joy may be complete. (1 John 1:1-4)

Contents

Foreword	ix
Acknowledgments	xi
INTRODUCTION	1
Transcriber's Prologue	3
Tributes to AD	9
THE MAN AND HIS FAITH	9
THE MAN AND HIS INFLUENCE	11
The Process of Communication	13
MARGARET FLAVELL—CLAIRVOYANT	13
DISCARNATE TO INCARNATE	15
WHAT THE MEDIUM EXPERIENCES	20
THE MESSAGE	23
1 From Life, through Death, to LIFE	25
2 As I See It	31
3 We Are Reunited	34
4 Jesus, the Light	36
5 Easter from Beyond	39
6 The Planes of Existence	41
7 The Spiritual Bodies	44
8 Heaven and Hell	53
9 The Dynamic Substance of Thought	61

10	The Power of Prayer	67
11	Forgive Us Our Sins	73
12	Pictures from the Realm Beyond	79
13	Astral Libraries	85
14	Occupations in the Realm Beyond	89
15	AD Meets Some Theologians	91
16	No Measured Time	95
17	Personal Responsibility—Universal Responsibility	99
18	Reciprocal Worship between the Seen and the Unseen	106
19	Worship Research	115
20	The Universality of Truth	118
21	Mystical Experiences of Expanding Consciousness	122
	Epilogue from AD	129

APPENDIXES 131

1	Vita, Alvin Daniel Mattson—1895-1970	133
2	The "Evidential"	136
3	Man's Responsibility in Achieving Harmony in God's Kingdom: Quotes from AD's writings	145
4	Quotes from Hymns and Prayers of Christendom	147
5	Bibliography for Suggested Reading	150

Foreword

For a strictly orthodox theologian the reality of the world of the spirit is not even subject to debate; it is the true world of which ours is but the clouded mirror image. One cannot, day after day, say "therefore with Angels and Archangels, and with all the company of heaven, we laud and magnify thy glorious Name" without such an idea becoming dominant in the mind.

In the consistent practice of religion one becomes acutely aware of what may be termed "influences"—all those strange bits of precognition, the knowledge of important events taking place in far-removed places, the curious distinction between a "happy" house and an "unhappy" one, panic, fear, an inexplicable sense of horror, et cetera. All these argue for senses other than the exclusively material ones. They may be apprehended by agreed-upon symbols, such as the cloud in Holy Scriptures or the raven flying back and forth over the cross on the dome of St. Paul's, or they may be objectified in some other form that the individual will find credible, such as a dream or vision. The more sophisticated the person, the less will be the degree of objectification. The methodology is quite unimportant for all that matters is the authenticity of the message. Is it true?

In the matter of communication between the realm of spirit and the realm of matter, we doubtless often make distinctions that are meaningless. How does one hear a nonvoice? In what form does a spirit have to disguise itself to be known to us? To what degree does the personality and mentality of the medium unconsciously distort the communication? The most distinguished clairvoyants I have met are hypersensitive about the too-easy charlatanism of the professional "mind reader" type. That someone who has never seen me before can tell me what my father looked like leaves me totally unimpressed—that can be drawn directly out of my mind. It may prove something about ESP, but it proves nothing about my father.

When someone who has never met me starts producing my father's thought form on a subject he and I never discussed, I am impressed. Thought form is for me as unique as an individual's handwriting. For example, I would recognize Bishop Manning's thought form on any subject. I mean exactly that. My criteria for the credible communication of personality are thought form and unexplored thinking.

What emerges from this book is a consistent, highly original mind. AD's descriptions avoid every cliché in this field. The utopian approach to another world is never evident. The handling of visibility and recognition could have been dictated by Gregory of Nyssa. The nonsentimental handling of a serious pastoral problem sounds totally unlike any bit of sweetness and light ever uttered on the subject.

I have met both AD's daughter and the clairvoyant involved. They are charming, intelligent women. You must believe me when I say that neither has a mind even remotely similar to AD's. In complete honesty I should even have to say that his message, reported with scrupulous fidelity, every now and then seems to cross purposes with his daughter's understanding of it. This conforms exactly to my criteria, therefore I am impressed.

The Reverend Canon Edward N. West
Sub-Dean of the Cathedral Church
of St. John the Devine
New York, New York

Acknowledgments

My sincere thanks are offered to all who have assisted me in preparing this manuscript.

Special appreciation is expressed to the Reverend Canon Edward N. West for the Foreword; to the Reverend Doctor Hjalmar W. Johnson and to the Reverend John A. Nasstrom for their tributes to AD; to the Reverend Canon Berton S. Levering for his introductory comments about Margaret Flavell; to the Reverend Allen C. Nelson for his permission to quote from AD's funeral sermon; to all of the friends who took the time to read the manuscript in order to give helpful suggestions; and especially to William H. Gentz of Hawthorn Books for his editorial guidance.

My very special thanks go to my husband, Harold V. Taylor, and to our son, Bruce M. Taylor, for their patient and continuing help in the editing process.

I am also grateful for the following permissions to use copyrighted material:

To the Division of Education and Ministry of the National Council of Churches of Christ in the United States for permission to quote from the *Revised Standard Version Bible,* (copyright 1952).

To the Board of Publication of the Lutheran Church in America and the Knubel-Miller Foundation Lectures to quote from A. D. Mattson's book, *The Social Responsibility of Christians* (Philadelphia: Muhlenberg Press, copyright 1960). 1960).

To the Board of Publication of the Lutheran Church in America to quote from *The Service Book and Hymnal* of the Lutheran Church in America (copyright 1958).

To the Parapsychology Foundation, Inc., for permission to quote from the Parapsychological Monograph by Dr. Lawrence LeShan, *Toward a General Theory of the Paranormal* (copyright 1969).

INTRODUCTION

Transcriber's Prologue

On March 2, 1971, an unexpected and unusual project began to evolve. The essence of that project is revealed in this book.

My father, the Reverend Alvin Daniel Mattson, S.T.D., a Lutheran theologian, died on October 19, 1970. Affectionately known as "AD" by hundreds of former students, colleagues, and friends, he was a pioneer among the clergymen who sought to awaken the organized church to its responsibilities in the area of social justice.

Not quite five months after AD died, Margaret Flavell, a close friend from London, was visiting us. She is one of the most respected clairvoyants in England and has a remarkable record of accomplishments in the field of psychic communication. On the morning of March 2, 1971, we decided to see if we could get in touch with AD from the world beyond and to tape-record our attempt. We had expected to make contact with him and to get evidence that he does survive, but little did we expect the quantity and quality of very significant communication and information that we received. From

March 1971 through October 1973 we received fifty-five communications amounting to over five hundred legal-sized pages of typed transcripts. For this book we have extracted the material we felt would be of interest to the general reader. Communications of a very personal nature, relating to our immediate family, have been deleted.

AD always believed that truth, wherever it is found, is universal. In keeping with this belief, this material is intended for all men, whatever their religious or philosophical beliefs. A widely respected theologian, AD speaks through the chapters of this book, bringing us his message from the spiritual world.

Throughout his life AD stressed that the Kingdom of God is the sovereignty of God embedded in the very nature of reality. In the prophetic tradition of Jesus and the Old Testament prophets, he taught that when man and society are oriented with the laws of the Kingdom, they function in an integrative, constructive way, thus experiencing the wholeness and "Shalom" that God intends for them. This AD continues to stress from the realm beyond, relating the truth he finds there to our world here.

He states, "We shall attempt to convey everyday revelations that will help take people the next step on their pilgrimage within the Kingdom of God. We want them to know more so that they can live life more fully. Knowledge about life everlasting can make the living of every single day on earth an exciting, new adventure."

Even though the Bible contains much evidence that the paranormal is part of God's activity, too many churches have ignored this whole area. As a result, many people believe that anything paranormal is "spooky" or even evil. They often relate it only to the misdirected use some people have made of the occult, extrasensory aspects of experience. Scientific studies throughout the years have supported the biblical evidences of survival. AD often was distressed that so many people were closed to this evidence, which could have opened broad new horizons for them.

Pierre Teilhard de Chardin, the priest and scientist, stated, "A new domain of psychical expansion—that is what we lack. And it is staring us in the face if we would only raise our heads to look at it."[1]

The religious nature of the paranormal is emphasized by AD throughout, helping to place the paranormal in a proper perspective. It then becomes an important adjunct to faith and a reinforcement to doctrinal belief in survival. The Gospel of Matthew reminds us that *we can know*. "Ask and it will be given to you; seek and you will find; knock and it will be opened to you. For every one who asks receives, and he who seeks finds, and to him who knocks it will be opened." (Matthew 7:7-8)

This book presents AD's first impressions when he passed over and basic concepts of the realm beyond, as related by him through the mediumship of Margaret Flavell.[2] The down-to-earth concerns with which AD deals show the intimate interexistence of God's realms. Far from being "otherworldly," the topics he speaks about are "interworldly."

There are many theories as to the sources of material brought through to us by mediums. Some suggest mediums tap knowledge from their own "higher selves," or tap a "world mind-pool of knowledge," or tap a "universal mind," or have telepathic reception from a sitter or direct communication from a discarnate person. In this book we are not attempting to prove or disprove any of these theories. We are

---

[1] Pierre Teilhard de Chardin, *The Phenomenon of Man* (New York and Evanston, Ill.: Harper & Row, 1961), p. 253.

[2] A medium is a person with special psychic gifts through whom communication apparently is made between the living and the dead. The voice on the tapes is that of Margaret Flavell, relaying the communication given her by AD. Background material on Margaret Flavell may be found on p. 13.

simply presenting what has been a most relevant experience for us. The reader will have to draw his own conclusions after analyzing the contents.

A sensing of truth in mystical areas often comes by direct insight—as indeed does faith in God. From what we have experienced, I am firmly convinced that AD survives and that, with the training and help of others in the realm beyond, he has been given the privilege and opportunity to communicate to us a vision of the "beyond" to give our lives more meaning here. AD's colleagues and students who have heard the tapes also have been quick to pick up the nuances of his personality and other evidential material, further reinforcing my own strong conviction.

Margaret Flavell and AD never met while he was on earth, making the evidential material of the communications, as well as the nuances of his personality that come through, all the more significant.

Evidential material that gives substantiation to the identity of the communicator is presented on pages 136-144. Regarding the evidential, some parapsychologists may pose the possibility of telepathy from the sitter to the medium. There is no way that the functioning of telepathy can be proved, or disproved, as far as these communications are concerned. I simply state that, from what I experienced, I feel the functioning of telepathy is very *un*likely. The evidential material came through during the sittings with surprising unexpectedness. This spontaneity has been very evident to all who have heard the tapes. I can attest that there certainly was no conscious telepathy on my part. Due to the rapidity of the communication, some of the material did not even impress me as evidential until later, during the process of transcribing, when I became aware of its significance. For Margaret to have probed my subconscious mind for the evidential during the nonhesitating, easy-flowing communication would be a feat far more remarkable than the relaying of direct clairaudient communication from AD. Also, there was some evidential material that could not, *under any circumstances*, be attributed to telepathy, either conscious or subconscious.

We cannot hope to grasp fully some of the material concerning concepts of the realm beyond since it comes from a realm of experience that is not yet ours. Each reader will have to interpret and accept according to his own understanding. For those unfamiliar with parapsychological literature, we have included, in the appendixes, a suggested bibliography for additional reading, which may make some of the concepts presented in this book more clear to the reader uninitiated in this field.

To the many people who are seeking reassurance for their doctrinal belief in survival, we hope this book will be of help.

RUTH MATTSON TAYLOR

Tributes to AD

THE MAN AND HIS FAITH
by the Reverend Dr. Hjalmar W. Johnson
*Professor Emeritus in History and Philosophy of Religion
Lutheran School of Theology, Chicago
and former colleague of AD*

As a member of the Communion of Saints, AD affirmed his living hope and faith in God and in the life everlasting. In glad obedience to that hope and faith he responded to the Lord's appeal as expressed in the Gospel according to John, "Believe in God, believe also in me. In my Father's house are many rooms." It was AD's conviction that abiding trust in the God of love and justice and power is ultimately blessed with the God-given assurance of eternal life.

Faith in eternal life did not mean for AD any type of otherworldliness that induced neglect or disrespect for divinely established values and duties of the present life. Nor did AD believe that responsible concern and faithful and wise action in things temporal would weaken man's faith in God's eternal world.

With a humble and thankful heart, AD entrusted himself to a faithful Creator who cares about his creation and "is not far from each one of us."

AD's deep faith in survival, rooted and grounded in his trust in God through Jesus Christ, did not cancel the priority of worship in his life. It did not lead him to slight the other areas and concerns of dynamic faith. Nor did AD regard his assurance of survival as justification for a negative attitude toward all the phenomena of parapsychology. On the contrary, he believed that psychic phenomena, under whatever name they are subsumed, should receive increasing scientific study leading to just evaluations of conscientious work in these significant fields. AD's interest in parapsychology developed strongly during the time of his graduate studies at Yale University Divinity School, and it continued to grow throughout his life.

When the revered Pastor Olof Olsson was writing his book, *The Christian Hope,* he came upon a book containing letters that were represented as having been communicated by a departed friend to a surviving friend. Dr. Olsson was so deeply impressed by these materials that he included a brief summary of their contents in his own book together with this explanation: "The contents seem to me to be so beautiful that I cannot refrain from sharing a summary for the comfort of those who need the same reassurance as I do. Read and receive from it whatever you desire and are able to receive."

In publishing her thoughtful account, Ruth Mattson Taylor is also saying, "Read and receive from it whatever you desire and are able to receive."

THE MAN AND HIS INFLUENCE
by the Reverend John A. Nasstrom
*Executive in the Division of Mission and Ministry
Lutheran Council in the United States
and former student of AD*

Remembering A. D. Mattson is to remind yourself of the influence of the man. Like hundreds of others who attended his classes in theological seminary, my thinking has been significantly shaped by exposure to AD's thought and ideas. Not many of us were aware of his interest in paranormal experience. I, for one, have been too busy wrestling with the here and now. But a recent budding desire to know more of the nature of the afterlife may mean continued contact and influence from AD.

Some readers of this book, especially those who knew AD as a professor of social ethics, may wonder about the connection between his social concern and his interest in the life beyond. The inclination is to think that people committed to solving the problems of society deal lightly with matters of a personal nature. But AD was a man deeply concerned with the personal as well as the social. As *Christian Social Consciousness,* one of his books, indicates, Christian social concern is a matter of consciousness. His was a faith active in love, the most profound definition of social ethics.

AD influenced his students to view man and society as a whole. He introduced us to the problems of rural communities

11

and early raised environmental questions that are being taken seriously today. With the same prophetic vision he called us to deal with industrialization and urbanization as they affect people. We were encouraged to "enter the stream of life," as AD put it. This we have done, not only in the classroom but on the picket line, in conversation with labor and business leaders, and in the organization of communities.

I recall AD's frequent emphasis upon the concept of the Kingdom of God. It occupies a central position in both the teaching of Jesus and the New Testament. I believe the idea of the Kingdom of God relates to my religious experience. I live out the life of faith in the context of a Reign of God that embraces the totality of human life. Concern for my soul's welfare is part of a concern for the welfare of all life. Only a comprehensive religious conceptualization like the Kingdom of God can satisfy my soul. What a legacy from AD!

There is a natural connection between sensitivity toward life and sensitivity toward the question of death. How natural, when understanding that the issue of life includes concern for its social dimensions, to also view death from a social perspective. It is true that each dies his own death. Yet do we die alone? The writer of Hebrews affirms, "we are surrounded by so great a cloud of witnesses" (Heb. 12:1). The readers of this book are privileged to learn of a unique man's experience of dying. He did not die in isolation. It was at the same time intensely personal and sublimely social.

Heretofore belief in survival after death has been largely a matter of intellectual assent to doctrinal statements about eternal life. Increasingly, we are being presented with material from human experience, communicated through sensitive people. Serious attention is being given to this paranormal material, often from a scientific approach. I find the evidence, although received from others and not from personal experience, too commanding to be ignored. Such is this book. AD's influence continues.

The Process of Communication

> Now there are varieties of gifts, but the same Spirit; and there are varieties of service, but the same Lord. . . . All these are inspired by one and the same Spirit who apportions to each one individually as he wills. (I Cor. 12:4,5,11)

Margaret Flavell—Clairvoyant

To experience a sitting with Margaret Flavell is to become convinced of the marvelous gifts with which she is endowed and of her integrity and dedication. The Reverend Canon Berton S. Levering, Rector Emeritus of All Saints Episcopal Church in Detroit, a man of outstanding repute who has known Margaret for many years, says of her:

> Margaret Flavell is a brilliant translator of thought communication from the world of the departed. Her early training in the London School of Paranormal Psychology and Sanctuary of Healing established a foundation of expanded spiritual awareness that has continued to grow. One feels her integrity of mind and deep sense of responsibility as she makes known the continuity of life. Her common sense, humility of spirit and dedication, illuminated by a fine sense of humor, enable her to share her experience with others.

I first met Margaret Flavell (Mrs. Edward Tweddell) on April 26, 1966, at the home of a mutual friend in Rye, New York. My mother had died in November 1960. There in Rye, on that day, through Margaret's mediumship, I had my first contact with my mother, as well as with three other deceased relatives who were with her. It was my first such contact with anyone from Beyond—a meaningful and uplifting experience. The evidential material was outstanding. Margaret knew nothing about my family and had never before met me, yet the evidential material that came through was indisputable.

Some of that evidence, surprisingly, dealt with china dishes. (I had always thought that contact with the Beyond would be of a very profound nature.) Through that sitting I learned that our personalities do not change much when we die. My mother had always treasured her collection of fine china, which was still at our home in Rock Island, Illinois. She expressed great concern that the dishes might be broken and told Margaret that I should have *certain specific pieces* shipped to my home in New York. Also, she told us of a beautiful cut-glass vase (of which I knew nothing) in a cupboard in my father's house in Rock Island. She wanted this vase made into a lamp for my brother and his wife. My father and I located the vase in the cupboard, exactly where she said it would be, and it now stands as a beautiful lamp on a table in my brother's home. (In our first sitting with AD, after his death, he told Margaret that he found it easy to communicate with her on the "thread" of communication that had been made first by my mother in Rye.)

Over the years I have come to know Margaret not only as a gifted clairvoyant but as a close friend. A Methodist by background, she is a deeply religious person. She uses her special abilities to help others deepen their faith and to become more God-centered.

Margaret is well known and respected among psychical research people in England for her accomplishments in that field. A born clairvoyant, she was highly trained over many years in the control of her natural psychic gifts through daily controlled experiments and disciplines. A graduate of the London School of Paranormal Psychology and Sanctuary of Healing, she later was assistant to Dr. Mona Rolfe, founder and director of the school.

Margaret is one of the rare positive mediums who receive while in full control and not in trance. During the Second World War, at the request of Lord Hugh Dowding, Marshall of the RAF, she and Dr. Rolfe collaborated in psychometry to trace many missing fliers, both alive and deceased, with a high degree of accuracy. (Psychometry is clairvoyance in which an object belonging to a person is used to aid the clairvoyant process.)

A very down-to-earth person, Margaret has been a teacher of English and foreign languages. This experience helped to create a fine vocabulary that is extremely useful in receiving communications. She also has worked in publishing, printing, and market research, and now combines a busy family and social life with her work as a lecturer and spiritual counselor and healer.

AD was very interested in the communications I had received from my mother through Margaret and had wanted to meet her. But as we have mentioned, *Margaret and AD never met while he was on earth,* which has made the evidential material of AD's communications, as well as the nuances of his personality that come through, all the more significant.

Margaret is a highly intelligent woman with a good sense of humor, which has made her an ideal match for AD in communicating with good rapport.

Discarnate to Incarnate

The reader might ask why AD, of the many theologians who have died, is able to communicate hundreds of pages of

15

material while others have only gotten scraps of information through. I think there are several reasons.

First of all, AD had a great desire to come back and share experiences with us. On numerous occasions he commented that when he died he was surely going to try to communicate back to earth. In many of the sittings it has been indicated that it requires a lot of discipline and training for him to do this.

Second, AD and I were very close when he was on earth. We were both deeply interested in psychic research and had frequent, lengthy discussions about developments in that field. Margaret and I also share a close friendship and respect. These ties, I'm sure, are a big factor in the ease of communication we experience.

Third, AD may be given the privilege of communicating extensively because, although he was highly educated in theology, he was always able to relate well to all people. This is one of the virtues of communications received from him: They are simply stated in easily comprehensible language.

Some readers of the manuscript felt we should include a description of the sittings when we taped the communications.

During a communication session, usually only Margaret and I were in the room. (Another close friend was present on a couple of occasions.) We would set aside a specific time to have a sitting, sending a thought to AD that we would be ready at that time. At the appointed time we would sit quietly in the room, beginning with silent meditation. When AD had arrived and was ready to communicate, he often would begin with a prayer such as, "Let the words of my mouth and the meditation of our hearts be acceptable in thy sight, oh Lord, our strength and our Redeemer."

Once the communication began, I, as the listener, would continue to sit silently and monitor the taping process. As mentioned earlier, Margaret is a "positive" medium and does not need to go into trance. It is as though she were relaying a phone conversation. It is Margaret's voice that is recorded on the tape, although changes in character of voice can be perceived when different communicators come through. The earliest sessions were about half an hour long as that was the duration of time AD was able to "hold" the line of communication. Now that he is more accustomed to communicating, sessions run as long as forty-five minutes to an hour.

The following material presents excerpts from various sittings through which AD attempted to give us some insight into the process of communication, as he sees it.

Visible Auras

In our very first sitting, when contact was made, AD stated, "Margaret, I see you as a combination of many colors, and I know I am communicating to you. I see you as a gray shape with flashing colors around you.[3] When you two were in silent meditation at the beginning of the sitting, the colors of both your auras (see chap. 7, p. 44) began to come down into regular bands. When they became a little still and only vibrated a little, that was the signal for us to begin to communicate. I was told to wait. If I prematurely rush in, I get a word or two through but then there is not a continuous, harmonious communication.

[3]When listening to the first tape, a parapsychologist wondered about AD's comment on seeing Margaret as a gray shape. Margaret and I were talking about this in January 1972 before a sitting. AD had overheard our conversation, and in the sitting that followed he said, "You made me smile when you spoke about that young man with his 'What is that about a gray shape?' You made me smile because many people see us as gray shapes, ghosts, apparitions. Therefore, why should he feel surprised that we might see you in the same way that you see us?"

However, there evidently is a gradual development of astral sight, which later enables those in the astral world to see the physical bodies of those on earth more clearly. On October 6, 1972, AD said to us, "Now, my children, I want you to know that I am beginning to see the bodies of people on earth very clearly."

"With Ruth I can see much green and blue, a great deal of blue and a mass of rose pink. The rose pink comes out like big flower petals, like big spiky dahlia petals, like funnels. That is your affection and your love going out. This you must not spread too far and wide, too frequently, without asking for the Lord to replenish you."

Light of Body

On another occasion AD remarked, "Margaret, you know what it is like to be light of body because the minute we begin to communicate with you, you lose your sense of heaviness of body."

Margaret then said to me, "You know that is absolutely true, Ruth, and I've never had anybody else describe it to me. I do feel that way when I've got a good communication. I'm not aware of how heavy my legs are, and if I move my legs, they feel as if they are going to float off somewhere and the feet will go off from the end of them."

AD then continued, "You, Ruth, could take this as a measure for yourself. When you have lost the feeling of the weight of your body, then you know that you are getting your inner self. I haven't yet become accustomed to all the words, the jargon concerning communication, so I'm trying to keep it simple."

As Winding a Skein of Wool

Again from AD, "A good receiver is one who, as though winding a skein of wool, keeps one end and winds it up carefully, carefully, like that tape is winding—listening and not allowing any thoughts to come in except what is actually being given to her by the communicator. The early mediums did not have the control of the brain and their mind, and they were unable to pass it over and allow it just to come in. That is why there had to be trance mediumship."

Thought Projection

In yet another sitting AD stated, "One of the real reasons for a great deal of frustration is the fact that I can only send a thought to Margaret, and she must translate that thought into words. As you are aware, I have stopped her on more than one occasion so that she will pick up the right word to interpret what my thought and meaning is. I am projecting my thought to Margaret without using words because it is slow and laborious for me to use words.

"It is vitally important for you to realize that, when you get a message, you should not condemn it and say 'But that's not his speech. That's not the way he talks.' I am not talking words. I am sending a thought from my mind to Margaret's mind, and her personality and brain have to interpret it."

The Stream of Life—the Holy Spirit

AD has sensed the undergirding of the Holy Spirit in the whole communication process, and he stated, "We have to tell all people who mourn that they must be comforted because unless they are comforted, we can't get through to them.

"There is this stream of life, the Holy Spirit, and it is like a spring coming up. It comes up into the pool of your own consciousness. If your own consciousness is so turbulent, the spring as it comes from the ground is taken up with all this turbulence.

"If you take a still pool and you place a spring at the back of it, water would come from the spring and it would move through the pool so that all you would see would be currents moving through the water until they come to the surface.

"When we communicate, this is how you should feel—that the Holy Spirit is like that spring in you and you receive through the calmness of your own consciousness, your subconscious mind if you like, but there should be this feeling.

"If you can't understand it any other way, fill up a bath of water, and then on a faucet put a tube, and put the tube at the bottom. Now let the water into the bath and you'll see how it makes patterns as it comes up—patterns as it infiltrates in the stillness of the bath water.

"This is exactly how the picture seems to me as I look at you, Margaret. You have this stillness, and through the spring of the Holy Spirit I am communicating with you. This movement is made spirit to spirit, and these movements impinge on the brain and the brain coats them in words."

What the Medium Experiences

Margaret Flavell was asked if she would try to describe what she, as a medium, experiences during communication. She said that it was very difficult to translate the experience into words but she would attempt to convey it to us as well as she could. Her account follows:

"I relax completely, quiet the mind and brain, hold in 'stillness,' and disassociate from the physical.

"In the stillness, I become aware of a different vibration that is insistent and continuous in its feel.

"On questing, I become aware of receiving a thought that is foreign. This thought develops and I become aware of a projected personality. On inquiring, a name/personality develops and, as over a telephone, a reciprocal conversation takes place.

"At times a picture of the person comes, as well as the personality traits. For example, I have seen AD in various places—under a canopy, which he described; sitting on a chair in various locations (we discussed these), etc. The first time of meeting I saw him in his favorite checked shirt and flannel trousers.

"A continuous conversation, mind to mind, deepens until AD, smoothly as in a physical conversation, expresses his thoughts and feelings. Sometimes the feelings received have caused laughter or tears. The latter I can register and feel with him. This may be called empathy.

"The whole contact is on a mind-to-mind basis—no trance—for I never leave my body. I am aware of where I am—in a room or in a car. AD communicated some information to me in my car, in a parking lot at the hospital, and this information I wrote down on paper rather than recording it on tape.

"It is possible to accept the thought without being aware of the presence of the communicator as a person, but AD generally projects his whole personality while sending his thoughts, so that anyone hearing his recorded talk recognizes him. The effect is quite different from the reply one receives in asking a question of the ether, not sending it to any particular personality or mind—then the reply is in a flash. One may wait for quite a period of time for a communicator to come through."

THE MESSAGE

1
From Life, through Death, to LIFE

> ... I am continually with thee;
> thou dost hold my right hand.
> Thou dost guide me with thy counsel,
> and afterward thou wilt receive me to glory. (Ps. 73:23-24)

AD had been in full vigor, enjoying the early autumn at his cabin in Minnesota, when he suddenly incurred a ruptured artery in his stomach. Surgery was performed, and he lived for five days after the onset of his illness, dying on October 19, 1970. My brother Al and I were with him during those last days.

Nurses witness death frequently. The nurses who tended AD before he died wrote to me afterward. I will share portions of their letters because they reinforce my own deep feeling that AD's death was quite special and beautiful.

One nurse wrote:

> In the short time I knew your father, I could see he was a wonderful person. In all my years of nursing I have never seen anyone so prepared for death.

Note: Each sitting contained some information of a very personal nature, pertaining to the immediate family, and some information of interest to people in general. Therefore, we have combined information of general interest into topic chapters.

The nurse who was with him when he died wrote:

> I was singularly honored to have shared just a few hours of your father's life, and his passing on to his greater reward. I am certain that his memory will be with me all the days of my life, for only those who have lived beautifully can die as beautifully as he did.
> . . . I have thought of him one hundred times or more. I am sure my life will be richer for having "passed him on the Way."

In the middle of the second sitting on March 6, 1971, AD unexpectedly described in detail the experience of his death. This was the first time, in all Margaret's years of communication, that anyone had described the actual experience of death.

AD began, "Now I will tell you how it was. The last few days before I passed, I was coming and going, coming and going.

"I was definitely aware. You know, if you are half asleep, you can be aware of somebody coming into the room and you just don't want to wake up. You know they're there and you think, 'Oh, well, if I stay asleep they'll go away.' "

"In the beginning I was conscious of my mother, of my brother, and of my father around me.[4]

"I was conscious of going to other countries and other places, but I really didn't want to go. I wanted to stop where I was. That was the physical body holding me. I would come back and I would tell you where I'd been.[5]

---

[4] Al had felt "cold spots" in AD's hospital room. In parapsychological research he had been doing with a young medium from India, Al had measured actual drops in temperature during communication sessions when discarnates were around.

[5] AD had much out-of-the-body travel the last few days before he died. Each time he returned to his body, he would tell Al and me where he had been. He mentioned such places as Montana, Illinois, Iowa, and even England.

"I was very aware of you and Al there with me in the room. It was good to have you there. I needed you.

"There was this tug between going and staying, and going and staying. As I went more and more, I loathed more the coming back. I felt regretful to leave, but I felt shut in when I got back. But not truly shut in because I wasn't properly in my physical body. I was partially in and partially out. My body became a very uncomfortable vehicle. It became very clumsy. My feet were so clumsy. I didn't feel as if I could move my feet somehow. They were like heavy clogs. They didn't feel like feet.

"Then the rest of me began to feel heavy like that, and it was an effort to lift my arm up. It was an effort to turn my head. I began to feel as though I didn't have enough effort. But it was so easy to go out and be out there. There was no effort to do that.[6]

"Then I thought that I really must stop this business of seesawing. I looked up in the air, and I saw something like a seesaw. And it was *hard* to put myself down and it was easy to stay up.

"Suddenly it became borne in on me that I had to make a decision. We all have to make the decision, really, whether we are going to struggle or whether we're going to let go. This is why people are afraid of death. The people who lack positiveness fear death even more because they dither, 'Shall I or shan't I?'

"I felt there was much I'd left undone, but it was pointed out to me there wasn't much I could do with a body like that anymore.

"My logical mind began to take over and I found myself saying, 'No, leave me now. It's enough. It's enough.' I wanted

[6] When I was at his bedside the day before he died, it was obvious that he was analyzing what he was experiencing. He had reflectively looked up and, as if to himself, asked the question, "Are we aware the mechanism is dying?" And then he proceeded to answer his own question, "Yes, we are aware the mechanism is dying."

to get the woman out of the way." (AD had asked his nurse not to tend him anymore but to stand aside and leave him alone to die.)

He continued, "Then I had this magnificent, wonderful vision. There were the gates. I had always envisioned that the entrance to my paradise would be through these magnificent gates. They're gates of life—of light. They're living gates. They're moving all the time. They're not wrought iron or stone or wood. There was this beautiful gate opening, and there were all of my family coming backward and forward to greet me.

"I said, 'Do you always have to go through gates like that?' And they said, 'No, this is because this is what *you* have always thought, and will have what you have imagined. You built this. This is yours—the gateway—your entrance of light. You can have St. Peter, if you like.' At that I had a little chuckle. I really didn't mind whether I had St. Peter or not. I said I perhaps could do without St. Peter.

"But then, as I turned my head slightly and looked, I saw a figure I knew was St. Peter. I said, 'I'm coming, I'm coming.' He said, 'Take your time, take your time. There's all the time in the world.' I thought, 'There isn't, you know.'

"Then I saw them. They came back. My family. They came back, and I looked at them. I no longer saw them as I'd seen them—like my children. They were no longer my children. They were souls that I had been blessed enough to provide bodies for. And I cried and I said to myself, 'Lord, thank you. I'm ready to go.' They tiptoed in and they looked at me. I didn't see them with my physical eyes. I saw them blurred.

They said, 'Are we holding you back?' They were asking, 'Shall we go and leave him or shall we stay?' I couldn't really tell them whether I wanted them to stay or go. I just thought it was beautiful to have them there."

At that point in the sitting I couldn't help weeping. AD said to me, "Don't cry, Ruth. You didn't cry then. What are you crying for now?" (I had held back my tears at his bedside when he died, as I didn't want tears I might shed to hold him back in any way.)

AD then continued, "I looked, and as I began gradually to leave them I had the most beautiful sensation of the complete unity with all things and all people. Margaret, I had a most beautiful passing, a most *beautiful* passing. I was conscious all the time. I thanked God for the body that I'd had, the opportunity I'd had, the children, and the gladness of the fact that my family and my wife were there waiting for me.

"And yet, you know, just a little bit of me said, 'Now come on AD, come on now, make up your mind, make up your mind, stop drifting.'

"And I felt some hands take me and lift me. And someone said, 'Come on, stand up, what are you lying down there for? You don't want to stay there all day, do you?'

"Well, the rest seems to be just light and sound and music, and the looking back, and the sending my love, and going around to the back of my children and just putting my hands on them. I went.

"I think I must have slept a bit because I don't remember. I remember coming through the gates and hailing Peter and a few other people, and suddenly I was in the most beautiful garden, sitting in a chair. They were all saying, 'Let him have a rest. He must rest. He must have a sleep.'

"And I was saying to myself, 'Rest, sleep—I've done enough of that. I want to get going.' But I didn't. Somebody must have hypnotized me because I slept and I rested. People came and went. I smiled at them and thought how beautiful they all were. They didn't have any faces. They were just a lot of light.

"Ruby came and she blessed me.[7] She said, 'Now look, they're having your funeral service. Do you want to go and look at it?' I said, 'Well, I don't know. I'm very comfortable.'

[7] His sister, who died in 1935.

And I really couldn't make up my mind. But my mind was made up for me because Ruth's dear mother, my dear wife, said to me, 'Well, I'm not going to miss it if you do. I just am not going to miss it. Come along and we'll have a look.'

"'I still was reluctant. I thought, 'Dear me, suppose they say something critical of me?' And my wife said, 'Oh, oh—you never did like criticism, did you? You haven't changed a bit.' Why did she think I would change—I'd only just come.'" (We had to laugh at that.)

Then AD said, "That's right, you have a good laugh. I had to laugh, and I said, 'Well, if I can stand up and if I can walk about and I can feel myself a man, a whole man, then I might go.' And we went.

"I really didn't know much at all about what arrangements they had made for the service, but it was all done very simply and very beautifully, just as I'd wanted it. I was doing a bit of eavesdropping as you, Ruth, and Al talked with people after the service, and then your mother said, 'Come, come, you've had enough. Come on.'

"I then went out into darkness, into the most beautiful, soft, enveloping darkness. The man I have learned is my guardian said, 'Come on, come on,' and when he says 'Come' it raises you and lifts you.

"I then had a nice, long sleep in a most beautiful bed in an arbor. And there was my lake and there were fish, but nothing like my cabin. It was most beautiful, light and airy.

"Well, here endeth the lesson.'"[8]

---

[8]In our liturgy the minister, at the close of the Old Testament reading, says, "Here endeth the lesson."

2
As I See It

> Why is it thought incredible by any of you that God raises the dead? (Acts 26:8)

AD expressed some thoughts to us on the significance of this communication project as he sees it. He stated, "We live and move and have our being in an immensity of power, light, and glory of God—such an immensity that we, as individuals, are only able to take one drop. We concentrate, and we receive on that drop.

"You, Ruth, will pick up and select a different wave band of understanding than Margaret or other people we know.

"If we are going to do anything at all with the material that I am being allowed to bring through, and I look upon it as a privilege to bring it through to you, then we must be aware that much we say will be old hat to some people. Much that you receive will be new, perhaps beyond other people. On the other hand, much will be just right for us. It is rather like that fairy story of the three bears. The porridge is too hot; the porridge is too cold; the porridge is just right.

"There is a tension that builds up in all incarnate people when they feel that they are verging slightly onto knowledge of something they don't know. It's like going to the sea for the first time in a year and you put your bare toe in the water to see what the water is like before you immerse the whole of you. Then there are the hardy souls who race down to the beach and go splashing into the water. They rise up and gasp that it's very cold. There are very few who will throw themselves into the sea of the Holy Spirit. Some merely put their toe in and tentatively feel it. The years of putting toes in are past, and the time has come to throw yourself in.

"Through 'inspirers' where I am, I am allowed to see and to know and to appreciate. It is from them that I understand and know that there is this very wide project and this very big thought, that this is something other people shall know.

"We are merely being used by a greater force—by God—to bring information through that will help those who are themselves primarily God-centered, but God-centered in a narrow sphere, and we hope to bring them out into a wider sphere.

"My intention is to build an overall picture of where I am now and what I am seeing now and what I am knowing now. Later I will know how I may interpret for you the underlying rules and laws and cosmic significance of the experiences I am now having.

"*One thing I want to emphasize very strongly, and I emphasize it all the way through—I am giving it as I see it, truth as I understand it.* I don't want to quote chapter, book, and verse. I don't want to give texts. And I don't want to say 'as Freud said,' or Jung or Wesley or anybody else. I want, if possible, to give as clear a picture as I can of conditions that I am encountering, from my own perspective.

"If the Queen of England passes over, she will see it from her point of view. If an Indian wise man or a Tibetan priest or anyone else passes over, he will see it from his point of view. So therefore I cannot dogmatize over what I am giving. I can't say, 'This is what it's going to be like when you come over.' I can only describe the conditions here, and you can choose how you handle them when you come.

"I am not presenting material for a scientific discussion. I am not presenting material for a theological discussion. I am trying to present material for the average person who wants to know. In these communications I want to try to speak in a down-to-earth, practical manner.

"It is my hope that people will ponder over what I am giving so that they may begin to reach out and to find in themselves that which they are going to continue to use here. They will then be spared some of the fumbling, testing, and trying that I see going on with people who come over here without such preparation. If only *one* person is so helped, when the time comes to step out of the physical body, that he can come fearlessly and begin immediately to work, to expand, to grow, and to understand, then our efforts will all be worthwhile. That will be more important to me than if ten thousand people read what I am giving and all say: 'Oh yes, I have an idea but it's a bit difficult and I don't know that I can do anything with it.' I would like to think of this whole project as a teaching course. I hope that it will be used to instruct and also to give a basis for meditation."

3
We Are Reunited

> Now if Christ is preached as raised from the dead, how can some of you say that there is no resurrection of the dead? But if there is no resurrection of the dead, then Christ has not been raised, then our preaching is in vain, and your faith is in vain. (I Cor. 15:12-14)

One of the fears that people have about death is that they may never see loved ones again. AD was quick to assure us that, when we die, we are reunited with those we love.

"My last words when I was in my body were carried forward to the first words without my body and I found myself saying to your mother, 'Well, where did you come from?' I was not aware of her until I had actually stepped out. She told me that she had been around me for a long time there in the hospital. Your dear mother is just as ever—ready to get me organized and comfortably settled. We have wonderful periods of time together. As the Bible says, there are no marriages in heaven, but the bonds of true love and affection we have had with people on earth still remain. These ties draw us together here—to share, to love, and to BE.

"All mothers are helpful, and my own mother has been tremendously helpful to me since I came over. She has not lost her sense of humor either. Humor is vitally important here because one should never take oneself too seriously. Should we say that by taking ourselves too seriously we can become depressed—or should we say that depression makes us take ourselves too seriously? Either way, according to your grandmother, it is a mortal sin. She is as slim as a young girl and beautiful. You know, they don't use any adornments over here, except themselves, and that shines through like a great and tremendous light."

AD's mother had been blind for the last seventeen years of her life. All through her life, and especially through the period of her blindness, she was a most gracious and beautiful person and a source of inspiration to all of us.

AD's father, the Reverend J. A. Mattson, died in 1943. AD said that his father also had been extremely helpful to him in learning to adjust to the conditions of the new life.

He said, "I didn't appreciate that Father could teach me one-pointedness the way that he has been teaching me. Over here we have classes to learn one-pointedness. In these classes Father helps me to realize that there is a homing beam—a beam on which, like homing pigeons, we home back in on a person. He is very useful. When I am beginning to flicker and am not making the trip right, he will caution me to keep my thoughts together. Although I could concentrate very well on earth, there were times when I could have one concentration going on and another lot of thoughts going on in the back of my head, like most earthly people. You can't have that here or you'll find yourself on the way to London and you will have landed yourself somewhere in New York because you've just thought of someone in New York."

My father had been with his sister, Ruby, his brother, Karl, and many other relatives and friends. He stated that when he first went over it was like an open house with everyone coming to greet him. Later he had many opportunities to gain knowledge of the varied activities of his relatives and friends.

4
Jesus, the Light

> For it is the God who said, "Let light shine out of darkness," who has shone in our hearts to give the light of the knowledge of the glory of God in the face of Christ. (2 Cor. 4:6)

AD's spiritual reception came later. In March 1971 he stated, "I have seen the Lord Jesus in all his radiance, in all his glory, but not immediately on arrival because then you are still with the dust and vibrations of your own thinking.

"When I first saw him, the light and the glory and the surging of power was *so tremendous*. It was like an avalanche of feeling over me. At the present time I just don't feel that I have found a way in which to describe what it was like—an indescribable contentment and uplifting, a tremendous ecstasy of feeling on all planes, being completely out of yourself, an unusually vivid knowledge of the intense, sympathetic love around you—the warmth of it, the light of it—something that is not external but is part of you. It is like a sunrise on a mountain that is covered with snow, when the colors come down and reflect on you—a dazzling brilliance that would make you close your eyes and yet feel it in every pore of your body. This is the feeling that you have as you come toward the LIGHT.

"And then suddenly to hear the voice that says, 'Look at me.' And when you look—there, just as you've always imagined—you see him. He shows himself to us according to our own understanding. If I want to think of him as a man who walked by the lake and a man who looked as the Jews looked at that time, then I'll see him that way. If in my thought I think he's modern and bright, then I'll see him that way. We do not see him as the medieval painters made him. We see him as we, in our own selves, have pictured him, because otherwise we wouldn't recognize him. How would we *know* unless we have the picture already in our own being—in our own minds, in our own hearts?

"To me he came walking across the air—across the tops of the buildings, the trees. I'd always known he'd come toward me with his arms and hands outstretched. He said, 'Come, let me show you'—because I have an insatiable curiosity and I must see and I must know. But there was no 'falling asleep in the arms of Jesus.' There was the knowing warmth of BEING that I've always known would be. It was so much beyond what words can tell.

"It is true that the Lord Jesus can take a form so solid that those who are in the body may see him—those who are in the dream state may see him and be called by him. But when I saw him *transcendent,* I was days and days just marveling and sensing and knowing. This was my *rebirth.* The body in which I now function was strengthened—made resilient, firm, aware. When I first came over here, I only knew what I had known and seen, shall we say, in a vision. But that was to see and not to experience. Until you have experienced it and been caught up without the ties and the cord that keep you with the physical body, it is very difficult to comprehend.

"Until you are released from the bondage of the physical body, you have no way of knowing the feeling and the uplifting and the thoughts that come into your head. The body is so much heavier than the personality which goes on. But even in your personality, there are times when you are completely detached—we call it a mystical ecstasy. Every time I turn my mind toward him now, I am engulfed in the power and time has no limits or meaning. It may be a flash, it may be hours—I know not. It is just a great *knowing*. I ask and he's there. He says, 'Follow me,' and we follow. But we don't follow with our feet. The whole being of you follows him because he is everywhere—in and through and around and *everywhere*. He is the manifestation of God."

5
Easter from Beyond

> And the Word became flesh and dwelt among us, full of grace and truth; we have beheld his glory, glory as of the only Son from the Father. . . . No one has ever seen God; the only Son who is in the bosom of the Father, he has made him known. (John 1:14,18)

On April 14, 1971, AD related the experience of his first Easter in the realm beyond.

"This festival of Easter has been a most uplifting experience. Here we continue to practice the rites of our respective churches, for on this plane we are conscious of our earthly personalities and modes of living. We are free to attend all services as we wish. The truly stupendous effect of all this worship is shown in the great streams of light and power and the various vibrations brought into being. Much of this ascends to higher levels. The light and love which are engendered on earth reach here and mingle with 'our' power. In rainbow-colored arches, this rises and descends, down into your vibrations in a continuous stream of molten light and wonderful sound.

"From Palm Sunday onward the heavier, darker colors became lighter. Then on Good Friday, into a midnight blue orb, the light began to spread. Gold and orange colors came through the deep blues and violets, each color adding its own sounds of music until Easter Day when that great beam of crystal light filled all the earth—ours and yours. It was quite impossible to remain alone, an individual. It was stupendous, mystical, wonderful, beyond the telling—until feeling became knowing and ecstasy beyond all speech.

"In the beginning was the Word—and here was the WORD—manifest, unmanifest,[9] awesome in manifestation. There was HE, the MAN OF GOD, JESUS HIMSELF, radiant in all his majesty and glory as a flower bursting from the bud, the leaf from the darkness of the sticky bud. Would I were able to paint this, portray this in sound. . . . One day according to your own understanding shall you all see as I have 'seen' and know as I 'know.' "

---

[9]We do not know exactly what AD meant by "unmanifest" but would assume that it means that the finite cannot *fully* comprehend the infinite.

6
The Planes of Existence

> This slight momentary affliction is preparing for us an eternal weight of glory beyond all comparison, because we look not to the things that are seen but to the things that are unseen; for the things that are seen are transient, but the things that are unseen are eternal. (2 Cor. 4:17-18)

Much literature deals with the concept of different planes of existence or levels of consciousness. Even the Bible refers to the *heavens* in the plural and, in 2 Cor.: 12, St. Paul refers to being caught up to the *third heaven.*

AD stated, "The world in which we find ourselves immediately after death we call the 'astral world.' From this point we can progress to higher planes—to higher levels of consciousness. By 'higher' planes I do not mean spatially higher but rather those planes which have a finer vibration.

"All of the various planes of consciousness have different frequencies of vibration. For instance, you assume that the matter of earth is composed of atoms and that these atoms are composed of energy which vibrates. This matter of earth is denser than the matter of the higher planes. As you can see light waves which vibrate at a 'visual observing' rate, so you can see the matter of earth. However, as you cannot see radio or television waves which vibrate at too fast a rate to be seen, so you cannot see the matter of the world beyond, unless you are clairvoyant.

"The spiritual bodies of those who have died vibrate at a rate too fast for your physical eyes to see. However, they can be viewed by clairvoyants whose sight has been opened to receive this faster vibration.

"You know, the world beyond is not up there somewhere. It's *here*—a change of condition. It is all in one space like a big sponge, containing all the different frequencies of vibration—like soapy water, salt water, clear water, the different densities of water—you can relate it to the different densities or vibrations that I have here. I can be soapy water and I can come down and see you. I can be salt water and I can stop on the mind level. Or I can be clear water and I can zoom through the mental plane[10] without any trouble at all. Someday I'll try to make it more lucid than that, but that is how it appears to me at the moment. You have to realize that I am a novice over here, very much a novice. But I must tell you that I know nearly as much as some of the oldsters who have been here a long while; I did my homework before I got here. The more you know about it when you are in the physical body, the easier it is for you when you get here.[11]

"However, I still have the feeling that I am 'up' somewhere and I am sending this 'down' to you. I haven't yet fully realized, as my teacher here tells me, that I don't have to project my communication downward. I just have to consider that I am sending it out from me and that it is being picked up at the same 'altitude.' I still have the feeling that I must thought-power it 'down' somewhere. You see, old ideas don't fade very fast.

"I have taken a number of trips out into the mental plane, and it is most interesting. You get there before you know it, whereas in the astral plane you are conscious of your going.

---

[10]The mental plane is a plane of finer frequency of vibration than the astral plane.

[11]AD had read widely in the parapsychological literature that had been published over the years and had a keen interest in the scientific studies undertaken in this field.

This is due to the difference in the rate of vibration of the two planes. For example, if you can send a thought around the world in no time at all, this can be compared to the mental plane. If you send a picture around the world, it takes longer than the thought—and this can be compared to the astral plane. In the astral body you are slower when you are moving, because you are moving through denser atmosphere—denser vibrations but not as dense as the physical world.

"The astral world is almost a replica of your world, except that it is of a finer substance and we are not 'bound' by our objective reality as you are.

"On the astral plane we are conscious of our personalities and the modes of life we carried out on earth. Therefore, we have denominations on this plane and we continue to practice the rites of our respective churches.

"On numerous occasions since I arrived here, I have been permitted to go into the higher planes where there is a unity of God-praise, not a segregation of the praise of God. However, I feel very strongly that there is work for me to do here, helping to break down the barriers which segregate the churches. Therefore, I shall be a sojurner on this astral plane but the higher planes, where there is a unity of God-praise, will be my spiritual home."

7
The Spiritual Bodies

> So is it with the resurrection of the dead. What is sown is perishable, what is raised is imperishable. . . . It is sown a physical body, it is raised a spiritual body. If there is a physical body, there is also a spiritual body. (I Cor. 15:42–44)

On numerous occasions, AD described the experience of functioning in a spiritual body. He stated, "I am now aware of the fact that man is composed of a series of bodies which interpenetrate each other. A proper body is provided for each plane of consciousness—each body composed of matter which vibrates at a rate compatible with the matter of the plane in which it was made to function.

"As I have told you, I have been permitted to go into the higher planes but am still able to return to my astral body on the astral plane. The process is similar to that experienced by man on earth when the physical body is in the sleep state and the astral body temporarily leaves the physical body to enter the astral realm, still attached to the physical body by a connecting cord of power.[12] However, when man returns to his physical body and awakens, he usually has no conscious recollection of these contacts with the astral realm during sleep, due to an etheric web between the physical and astral

---

[12] Clairvoyants see this connecting cord of power as a thread of light.

bodies, which blocks conscious recollection. Most people would not be able to function effectively in their daily tasks on earth if they were consciously aware of their astral experiences during sleep. It would be like trying to deal with two worlds at the same time. The experiences and knowledge man gains on the astral plane during sleep are stored in the subconscious and are drawn upon by him as he lives his life on earth.

"The same principle applies in going from the astral plane to the mental plane or higher planes, except that conscious memory is retained. For example, the astral body is left in a state similar to sleep and the mental body is then used to enter the mental plane. This same principle applies for all of the successively higher planes.

"When a person has fulfilled his purpose and development on the astral plane, he may then proceed permanently to enter the mental plane and the higher planes, in succession, to work and develop more fully there. In that case, the astral body is cast off, as is the physical body at death, and its particles disintegrate to be reused in the creative processes. However, a person who has gone into the higher planes in this way can still communicate through to earth and can still manifest himself on the astral plane through materialization."[13]

The Astral Body

"The astral body in which we live immediately after we have died is a duplicate of our physical body, except that it is made of a fine, tenuous substance. The creative power of God—the Life Force—radiates through and powers our spiritual bodies.

"We don't think of putting food into our mouths, because it isn't needed. Therefore, the whole of the astral digestive tract and the elimination organs, like the kidneys and colon, cease to function—I guess you could say they become

---

[13]See "Bodily Materialization from the Higher Realms to Lower Realms." chap. 9, p. 61.

paralytic. However, we continue to use the psychic centers of the body. These become much more active because they are now free of the physical body.

"These psychic centers, the chakras, are sources of spiritual energy and each has certain colors it contributes to the aura, or magnetic field of light which emanates from each person. There is an aura of light around the physical body which is visible to those, such as clairvoyants, who are attuned to see it.[14] There is also an aura of light around the astral body. The light and color characteristics of the aura of a person at a given time depend on which chakra or chakras are activated at that particular time. People trained in this area can often diagnose physical or mental disorders by the color of the aura seen. They can determine which part of the physical or emotional body is malfunctioning by the auric pattern and color which is evident. There are a number of books on this, and I would refer people to these other sources on the subject since I am not intending to give a scientific treatise here.[15] However, I do want people to be aware of this phenomenon of the glow of the magnetic field of each person and of the significance of changes in the appearance of the aura.

"Love, here, is experienced as a glorious mingling of the vibrations of the auric fields. (This, also, on occasion may be experienced while still in a physical body.) Loving widens

---

[14]Dr. Walter J. Kilner, *The Human Aura* (New Hyde Park, N.Y.: University Books, 1965), reports experiments using special colored screens to train nonclairvoyant persons to see the human aura. Sheila Ostrander and Lynne Schroeder, in *Psychic Discoveries Behind the Iron Curtain* (Englewood Cliffs, N.J.: Prentice-Hall, 1971), describe a machine the Soviets have developed that enables nonclairvoyant persons to view the human aura.

[15]Chakras, the psychic centers, are mentioned in writings of the Eastern philosophies. They are described as the centers through which the energy of the creative life force flows, charging the bodies of a person. Books on the chakras and auras are included in the suggested reading list in the bibliography on p. 150.

one's aura and field of contact and leaves a deep glow and warmth of affection.

"After death we see with the inner sight that is always within all earthly people. It is the same sight that is used when you sleep at night and dream. This is also the sight of clairvoyance. Clairvoyants are able to still the vibrations of their physical bodies, and they use this special sight to see the bodies of those in the astral world.

"The sense of smell is still with us. We can smell all the wonderful perfumes of the flowering trees and flowers.

"People who die when they are old can go back to a 'prime' age of life by a process of revitalization. Likewise, people who die at a young age can mature and progress to what they consider a 'prime' age."

In progressive sittings with AD, Margaret observed changes in his appearance. During the 1972 sittings she said that he looked considerably younger than in the 1971 sittings. In October 1972 AD said to me, "I want you to understand that I am now a middle-aged man again. I am not old anymore."

He also said, "The spiritual bodies are whole and perfect. Even a person who has lost a limb by amputation while in the physical body can function as a whole person in the spiritual world. The limbs of the spiritual bodies are not lost through amputation of physical limbs.

"However, people who have been physically ill for a long time on earth, or who have had a limb amputated before death, often carry that illness or disability over with them in their minds. They feel that they still have the disability in their astral bodies, and it is difficult for them to realize that they are whole persons.

"There are hospitals on the astral plane for the treatment of people who are not able to function effectively when they first pass over. The healers and physicians on the astral plane concentrate their treatment on making those persons realize that their illness is only in their minds and that the mind is influencing the astral body, producing a simulated illness.

"However, drug and alcohol addictions actually do carry over into the astral bodies. Withdrawal treatments must take place on the astral plane in these cases before a sense of wholeness can be achieved. It is *far* easier to break these habits while still in the physical body."

Travel by Thought

In April 1971 AD dictated a communication to Margaret in London in which he stated, "I grow stronger in mind directive daily and am still aware of day and night. I still utilize night for resting and meeting with all of you who still live in physical bodies. I presume that eventually resting need not mean 'sleep'—losing sense of self—but resting could be in the form of relaxing, meditating, listening to music, poetry, or fine prose, and thus recharging oneself.

"Vitality is required to propel our thinking. Eventually when we can 'think' ourselves to a desired place, we appear as a spark of light—a cometlike creature—or may even go out like a light and come on again at a desired place. This is an accomplishment and needs practice. Today I came in a horizontal position part of the way and then suddenly must have operated 'the law' and arrived in your room.[16]

"Here one can see small and large astral folks floating around or walking—on the ground then up a few inches, down again, up a few feet, and so on—all learning to use these astral bodies to best advantage. There are some who never go beyond a quick gliding walk for they wish to observe things and people around them as they go. They are the observers, the inquisitive ones. This is the mode I use when I go to visit new places or even revisit old familiar ones."

---

[16] As we understand from AD, the astral body can travel with the speed of radio or television waves and can penetrate earth matter.

Classes to Learn to Use the Astral Body

"As I have mentioned, there are classes here which one may join to learn how to use these astral bodies without the feeling of cumbersomeness that comes with the physical body.

"I have inquired into how Donna[17] was trained in her classes, and I appreciate that the way I have been trained is slightly different. In Donna's training she was led by her guide to a group of eight people and a leader. They would sit down, as if for meditation, and their guides sat with them.

"In the group Donna attended the members were told, after meditation and quietness, to extend a thought to each other in turn, beginning with the leader, and to get the feeling of empathy with the other. Then the leader began to make them appreciate that they were communicating with their thinking, without using their lips or words. Donna explained, 'I would try to say something to someone in my thinking. They would try to receive it and then say something to me.'

"In that group there were mixed levels of development. Some already were far along and communicating, while others were just beginning. Because of Donna's empathy with people, she found it quite easy and very quickly was beginning to pick up thought. She was then told to go to a certain room, and there she was to look on a shelf for a book. When she was standing in the room, she was to receive instructions by thought as to which book to take, which page to open, which sentence to read, and when to put the book back. Then she was to find her way back to the group by homing in, using swift thought and without walking on her feet. She described her difficulty of trying to walk in air before she could learn to home in without walking.

"It was then suggested that she should go and find someone out of the group in some other place. She was to find them by

---

[17] A friend of ours who died in 1968.

homing in on their vibration and bring a message back from them to the leader. In this way she was trained to go to a particular place and to come back, guided by the 'note' or vibration of a person."

On May 7, 1971, AD dictated a communication to Margaret in London, part of which dealt with orientation classes to learn to receive color. AD stated:

"Now, let us think of the easiest way to describe these orientation classes. In the group I attend there are eight of us and the teacher, in this case your friend, Donna. She is instructing beginners. We sit, relaxed, on chairs or backless stools. Upright. Hands on knees. We go into silence and then direct our attention on the leader. She is the 'broadcaster.' We are the 'receivers.' She projects colors, collects sound, and redirects them toward us. We sit in a widely spaced circle, almost a horseshoe shape. Donna projects the color, the sound. We tell what we have received. She advises if correct or incorrect. If the latter, we try again, remembering that we are to be passive and alert, switched on as a radio. I think the simile of a television set perhaps is more correct. We receive in color sometimes and in black and white on other occasions.

"This learning to receive color is one of the first exercises. To receive sound is the next step. I think I have told you that we have a note, a personal sound, which you in the physical body may hear, if properly attuned. This is the note used to attract our attention, to let us know when we are needed by anyone.

"Remember that color is sound and sound is color, so the exercise is a combined one. I understand this is not equivalent to the sounds made by earthly musical instruments, orchestras, etc. Many people on earth 'see' musical sounds as color, as you do, Margaret.

"So far, we are working on the holding of a color and listening for its sound, hearing notes and relating and seeing color. Quite a new field for me, so I am not too quick at it but will persevere.

"We leave the group in turn, and the remaining ones send out a thought, a call. We are listening as we walk about. Then, hearing it, we home in and return to the group, just as bees return to a hive when summoned, or a racing pigeon, released away from its loft, circles until it 'knows' the direction to home. It is necessary to become very familiar with this returning to base, for otherwise we could wander around, a lost soul. (If you think about that, we talk of lost souls as being divorced from God—yet no one is lost, not even a sparrow. They only think themselves lost.)

"It becomes easier to find one's way around when it's a repetitive action, and I'm doing quite well, but one must not get absent-minded."

Gradual Adjustments

AD told us that the astral plane brings truth to man on an emotional level, and he refers to the astral body as the "emotional body."

About fifteen months after he died, he said to us, "I am still using my emotional (astral) body. I haven't cast that off. I was not a highly emotional person, ever. I was quite practical, but you will be surprised what levels of the emotional body you retain with you when you pass over. If they have been a part of you, one retains compassion and love, understanding, a listening ear, and a certain amount of attention to detail. Such things as hunger and thirst, and going to sleep and waking up—those are cast off.

"I am still left with my inquisitiveness, my desire to know, my thirsting for knowledge, and my thirsting for new experiences. I'm still handicapped in a way by my liking old familiar things and ways. I was rather set in my ways, if I was not set in my thinking.[18] I had an orderly kind of daily routine, and this had to be forgotten. The fact that I expected to have

---

[18]These statements are true of AD and are evidential.

five or six hours of sleep a day and could sit down in a chair and doze—that still came through with me. It was a little while before I realized I didn't need the sleep. I didn't have to go to bed, and if I sat in a chair I didn't go to sleep. All these habits that we have on earth come through with us, and for a while we are subject to them. We must do these things because it is a shock to arrive here suddenly and to realize that certain things don't need to be done. This takes adjustment. I now have adjusted to the fact that I don't need to sleep, and I certainly don't need to eat or drink.

"If we're the kind of people who can't live without the written word and must know what's going on, then we're not going to be content to sit down and pick it up from the ether as the advanced people do. We must go and look at the printed word, visiting libraries and reading rooms. At first we communicate in words and find out how slow it is. That is the transitory stage before we start to communicate by thought. In all these ways one has to experiment. As I said before, in the beginning we have merely stepped out of the physical body and we are still ourselves. After a little while we begin to change and adapt to our new environment—the same way we change on earth by living in different areas."

8
Heaven and Hell

> I will give you the keys of the Kingdom of Heaven, and whatever you bind on earth shall be bound in heaven, and whatever you loose on earth shall be loosed in heaven. (Matt. 16:19)

Concerning heaven and hell, AD stated, "It is *not* true that when we die we wait for a judgment day.

"Heaven and hell are not places—they are spiritual states of being. They are not static states but are states in which there can be growth and progress toward ultimate wholeness of being.

"As there are degrees of heaven or hell on earth, so there are degrees of heaven or hell in the spiritual world. The spiritual state of being you have on earth is the spiritual state you take with you to the world beyond when you die.

"There is no sudden metamorphosis from an idle person into an active person, from a nonreligious person into a religious person, from a money-centered person into a God-centered person. This is not an automatic thing. Your personality—your likes and dislikes, your hopes, your fears—are still attached to you, although in a more nebulous form than when you are on earth in a physical body.

"I see people come over. They arrive and have high hopes that everything is going to be different for them. However, nothing can be different for them because they have brought with them what they are. There is so much harmony here, and if they have brought a disharmonious personality with them, they find it very difficult to link in with the harmonious existence that we have. This is something that grieves me when I see it.

"It is not true, as some people think, that if we only give verbal assent to belief in God, well, that's fine—that is our passport to heaven and everything will be all right. What we have to remember is that Jesus showed us the path by which it will be all right. He doesn't say, 'It's all right, Brother, come along in. Sit down now and relax and do nothing.' He says, 'It's all right. You are on my way. There are a lot of stones in it, but you are on my way. If you ask me, I'll help you over the stones.' The old teachings that 'as you strive, so you'll be helped' are right. The Lord helps those who help themselves.

"If you truly try to follow the laws of the Kingdom which the Lord has revealed, and ask for his help, he will aid you in becoming a whole person. As I see it from here, there is a rod of light—a pulsating power, the vital force of the Holy Spirit—right down through you. It is the self-centeredness of the personality which erects blocks and disturbances which make it impossible for the Holy Spirit to function through you. If you ask for help from the great physician, the Lord Jesus, he will help you to unlock the inner, healing power of the Holy Spirit which is within you so that it can be diffused and can spread throughout your being. The Lord will help you to achieve the attunement, the shalom, the peace, the wholeness which is heaven.

"Heaven is not sitting down and 'casting down your golden crowns' and singing 'Hallelujah.' However, I did notice that there is a tendency among certain sects or religious people over here to congregate in their little groups and have their little sessions of what they feel are 'heaven.' This is an interesting fact. I am told by my teacher here that eventually they become very bored with this narrowness, and *then* their own helpers and teachers here try to give them another thought and another idea and help them to break away from this narrow approach.

"We tend to feel that when we die, heaven is *as we thought it*—and it certainly is. As I've said, you can be received in exactly the same way you always thought you would be received. You may remain in that narrowness if you want —you need never change unless you wish. God gives us perfect freedom in spirit.

"The old notions are that you go 'up to heaven,' you go 'down to hell.' We have not understood that it is merely a matter of vibration. The finer the vibration is, the nearer we are to heaven. Heaven is a state of being joyous, light, loving, harmonious, vibrant, *God-centered and others-centered*. The heavier the vibration, the nearer we are to hell. Hell is a state of being heavy, dull, dismal, gray, and glum—as when you are heavily depressed and *self-centered*.

"People who have an orientation of hate, for instance, find themselves unable to appreciate a realm of love and harmony. Therefore, they continue in their state of bitterness and are 'closed' to the glory which exists around them. I am told by my spiritual inspirer that they have to wait. These people wait and gradually they appreciate the fact that it is very destructive to hate like that. When they have had real hates and have been emotionally upset like that, or have had a real bitterness toward someone, then it takes them quite a period of time to get the light and the power around them again, to be able to appreciate this place or that, or go to the Valley of Praise, or go and hear beautiful music. They just hear discords, and eventually they come to the realization that 'this isn't much of a life, is it?' And the moment that happens, those who are dedicated to work with this sort of person come and they have their methods of easing them away from the state they are in. It is like taking a skin off an onion. They will gently peel off this layer that is formed by hate—this shutting-in, restricting coat that comes on them with their violent, negative emotion.

"For someone who is bigoted and intolerant to come here when they lose their physical bodies, it is also a very painful and very uncomfortable life. It is very lonely. It is almost as if they are encased in a hard shell or hard covering and there is great difficulty in finding a chink or a crack and bursting out.

"If you are tolerant, sympathetic, and easily touched when you are on earth, you may find that your sympathetic tears and emotion for other people may make you a bit uncomfortable sometimes. You may feel a bit ashamed at having to blow your nose and dab the tears from your eyes, feeling that other people may not understand. However, you may have the consolation of knowing that when you get here, you will have less work to do because you will not have to undo and dispel and disintegrate a hard shell of indifference or intolerance.

"This plane is so full of different people, so many different people, that one must learn tolerance very quickly. Otherwise you meet someone and, if you are not tolerant toward them, you are immediately consumed by annoyance and your spiritual body becomes upset. You can get mental indigestion. You then need to go and find somebody to calm you down and sort you out. In the same way that you go to a doctor for an upset physical body, so you can go to a clinic or healer here and get your astral body sorted out. It is an odd sensation to go talk and be smoothed down, as it were. It always reminds me, when I watch it being done, of how a bird, a seagull in particular, will come down to land. Just as it touches water it is protected and buoyed, and the bird folds all its feathers and its wings down until it is smooth and sleek. This is exactly how our aura has to be smoothed down—until it is smooth and sleek."

Is There a Devil?

We asked AD if he could enlighten us about the existence, or non-existence, of a devil. He stated, "Just knowing the bad mistakes you made through your carelessness or your selfishness is a hell. You don't need a devil prodding you with a fork. Believe me, your own anguished mind is a prod that is more hurtful than any prodding with a devil's fork.

"I met a man over here who said that he would gladly exchange good old Dante's Inferno for the mental anguish he was experiencing over guilt feelings from wrong actions he had taken on earth in certain business matters. In Dante's Inferno he would be able to complain that the devil was doing this to him, whereas now he had no devil to complain of because the devil was himself.

"Whether there is a negative personal being who can be called the devil I cannot say. I have not seen anyone personified as the devil. There certainly is an evil force which builds up from the negative aspects of life and has a tremendous influence. Thought forms[19] which are evil certainly play a part, but I don't think they are the whole answer.

"The problem of evil is a very perplexing one. We have not solved it here, either. There is a negative aspect in existence which causes man to react contrary to God's will. What the original source of that negativism is, we do not know—only God knows. This is a theological question that has bothered man through the ages. If we get further thoughts on this, we'll bring them through."

The Depths of Hell

We were also curious about what happens to people who have been hardened criminals on earth, and asked AD about this. He stated, "There is a condition which could be termed

---

[19] See pp. 61, 62, 77.

the 'depths of hell.' People who have deliberately chosen to live debased or cruel lives and have turned their backs on the light of God find themselves in a state similar to groping in a dark and depressing fog. Everyone there is wrapped up in his own cruel thinking. These souls wander around in this lost state until they, of their own volition, make an attempt to turn toward the realm of light. Some may be lost for eons of time.

"There are souls called the 'shining ones' who dedicate themselves to going into this dark realm and bringing spiritual light. The souls who are dedicated to this work of rehabilitation are clothed in protective garments so that they are not harmed or pierced by the daggerlike thoughts of hatred which those in the dark realms are throwing out. The shining ones are not allowed to go and talk to these people, but they stand nearby and call to them through thought—prayer, if you like. The moment souls in this dark area respond in a positive way, the ones who have come to help are able to bring them out into a less dense, foggy world and eventually out into the realm of light."

Lower Astral States

"Some people find themselves 'earth-bound' after death. This is a lower astral state. For example, people who die suddenly by accident, perhaps when they are young, are often loathe to leave the earth as they feel a sense of incompletion of their earthly life. They stay close to the earth, 'haunting' the homes and places they have left. It is only through a process of education that they can be urged away from this unhealthy condition and helped to progress and grow in the new state in which they find themselves. Prayers made on behalf of these people from those still on earth can be a great support and help. These prayers help release them to go on and partake of the ever-expanding life in the world beyond.

"Persons who commit suicide before the time they are meant to die find themselves in a state of heavier vibrations and closer to the earth than those of us who died natural deaths. They remain in this state of density until the time when they would have normally died. They then may pass into the planes of finer vibration. People who have experienced death through suicide are greatly helped by the prayers and supportive thoughts from those still on earth. They are also aided by those from the higher planes who are dedicated to help them grow spiritually during the period of waiting.

"Among others, the lower astral planes also contain people who have been alcoholics or drug addicts, who find these cravings still with them in the astral bodies. They stay near the earth to be near alcoholics or drug addicts who are still in the physical body, in order to participate vicariously in the sensations which alcohol and drugs give. They can be helped in the world beyond to clear their astral bodies of these cravings so that they, too, may go on and progress. However, this is a long and tedious process.

"We have to try to convey to people still in the physical body that they can't expect a sudden change for the better. They must help themselves while they are on earth."

Drugs and the Dangers of "Back-Door" Knowing

"Drugs are a back door to knowing. Some mistakenly think they can take a drug to see what it is going to be like when they die. The trip they experience on drugs is not going to be anything at all like the experience after death. Feel sorry for those whose minds are in such a sad state that they have to take the back doors of life, when knowledge can be gained safely through the front door of sincere spiritual seeking through prayer and meditation.

"In addition to damaging the physical and astral bodies, there are grave dangers in taking drugs. As I said, there are many astral figures hovering around the drug users on earth. In this hovering around they vicariously participate with the drug user. They are linking in and, like leeches, they are experiencing what the earthly drug user is experiencing. If such a one attaches himself to a drug user, that drug user is in far worse condition afterward.

"You can see some of the drug users on earth sitting around in various states of hallucination. They have a very pathetic look as if they had no soul—vacant behind the eyes. Many times they actually are vacant. During a trip they may actually be out of their body, and temporarily it is just a shell that is sitting there, being motivated by the mechanical processes of the physical body. Often there are astral entities trying to get into that vacant body, and the drug user's guardian from the astral realm has a terrible battle trying to keep these astral entities from possessing the body of the drug user. This is a grave danger. There have been times when the wrong entity has slipped in, and then there has been great trouble in removing that entity so that the owner of the physical body can come back. This is always a grave danger if a person takes a drug which causes that person to vacate his physical body.

"We talk about pollution and cleaning up nature. I believe in cleaning up nature, but I also feel that we have got to start with cleaning up the nature in man. Man has got to face life through the front doors and not seek back doors into life's experiences."

9
The Dynamic Substance of Thought

> For though we live in the world we are not carrying on a worldly war, for the weapons of our warfare are not worldly but have divine power to destroy strongholds. We destroy arguments and every proud obstacle to the knowledge of God, and take every thought captive to obey Christ.
>
> (2 Cor. 10:3-5)

Concerning the creative power of thought, AD stated, "Things are not born in the astral world. They are created by thought. Thought is the essence of all things. Be careful that your thinking is not slipshod and formless, because when you come out of the body you actually meet the thought forms that you create in your thinking. Your thinking, praying, or inquiring goes out from you in waves. Nothing is ever lost—nothing is ever put aside or unused, even your thought."

Discipline Your Thinking

"We don't appreciate the wrenching that goes on when we begin to think about one thing and then stop that thinking and go to another. If we don't make a clear cut between one set of thoughts and another, it looks like a tangled skein of wool to anybody who is looking on.

"Disciplined persons have disciplined thinking. This is most evident when they arrive here. When they tackle a subject, there is no deviation, no intrusion, no obstacle. They think it out in a straight line and arrive at a point. The thinking patterns around them are regular, clearcut, and sharp on the edge. They know exactly what they are going to do, say, or think on a particular subject or line of thought.

"We sometimes meet souls who are not disciplined in their thinking. They just drift along, and it looks like a lot of cobwebs around them. You talk to them and they can't even finish a sentence in their thinking before they have bobbed off onto another. There is no adhesion, no cohesion.

"Learn to concentrate. Discipline your thinking. Learn to keep your mind on one topic at a time. Allow yourself to become immersed in it. This is a most useful attitude to develop for life when you are on earth, and it carries over with you when you come to the astral world."

The Importance of Right Thinking

"I have always enjoyed a good discussion, but here you cannot put out thoughts into the ether that you don't really believe as truth, just for the sake of provoking an argument or discussion. If we put such thoughts into the ether, we lose far more spiritual energy than it is wise to lose. We then have to sit back, be quiet, concentrate, and start drawing the power back again. This is retribution because you have to use power to withdraw an untruth from the ether. That power could be used for more constructive purposes. This applies to *all* negative thinking—here as well as on earth.

"When you are in a physical body, the negative thought forms you create stay right with you. In order to get rid of them, you have to nullify your negative or disagreeable thinking by positive thinking. Positive thought forms have to be created to remove the negative ones before you can feel right. This requires effort and concentration, which would not have to be expended if you had held a positive and agreeable approach to life in the first place.

"You know that even a rainy, windy day can get you off on the wrong foot, making you feel depressed, unhappy, and unable to function as your best self. Even this can be nullified by a proper attitude and by extending a thought such as, 'The earth needs all this water and the trees enjoy being blown. It doesn't really matter about me—I can put on a raincoat and boots and protect myself.' The attitude with which you approach such weather can make all the difference in the world as to your effectiveness as a person for that day."

Visual Patterns of Thought

"Until I left my physical body, I was not sufficiently aware that there were visual patterns of thought. This is something that would be interesting for people to know. Even the desultory conversation of a family around a meal table forms a pattern. When you find members of a family who are truly adjusted to each other and are enjoying themselves, there may be the most beautiful flower that is left as a thought pattern when they have finished their meal. When there is jangling and egotism of one trying to dominate the others, the one pushing in on the others will leave a thought pattern like tangled wire. There will be more solidity to it than from the ones who are passive, listening and perhaps just adding color and understanding or maybe a prayer.

"This is an extremely interesting area, and one on which those whom you might call your guardians from the astral realm can tune in. They tune in on a particular visual pattern, and from this they can interpret your need. A guardian never controls your action, but he can give you support for original thinking. He can try to guide an individual into his own pattern and way of thinking, which will be helpful.

"We do not go around indiscriminately spying into people's lives. However, someone may send out a call wanting to know, 'Now, what on earth should I do over this?' When they sit down to think about it, that sends out a great, huge question mark, and we know according to the color of that thought form the level of the question. For example, 'What shall I do about my bank balance?' gives us a sort of reddish color of trepidation with a little green and quite a bit of brown. That's not my color—I can't help them with money—but those who have been financiers and those who know how to deal in these areas will come. They will direct ideas and thought into the people's auras—into their physical magnetic field—so that they may pick up a book, open a newspaper, make a telephone call, or get in touch with a person who can help them with their problems. This is the way they are helped.

"I want to emphasize again, though, that there is a privacy around all people on earth which cannot be violated. Those of us in the astral world are not allowed to go around and see what is going on in a person's life unless we are called to do so by that person. I am allowed to go over the material I am putting through for you, after it has been given, to see the impression it has on you and the various people who are sharing it. However, I am not allowed to go around and see what is going on in the homes of people anymore than I could do that, uninvited, when I was on earth. The privacy of people is respected."

Materialization Through Thought

Thought as a creative force to materialize objects was mentioned by AD throughout the sittings.

Regarding clothes on the astral plane, AD stated, "When you come here, you experiment with your thinking and you think up your clothes. When I was on earth, a member of my family would say, 'You know, I think I would really like a green dress the next time in such and such a style.' And she, in her own mind, would have thought out the kind of dress she would want. Like a fashion designer, she would think out a style. Well, here you think up your clothes, they materialize, and you put them on. When you want to change what you are wearing, you can thought-power off the clothes you have on and create something else. We all tend to wear the kind of things that we enjoy. Most of us, in the beginning, wear the things to which we are accustomed."

Margaret also received "pictures" of thought-created buildings with vibrantly colorful mosaic floors and handsome furnishings. In one sitting she saw a beautiful azalea bush about ten feet high behind the area where AD was sitting. It had blooms of many colors, ranging from pale yellow to deep crimson, all on one bush. She questioned AD about the unusual azalea and how all those colors could be gotten on one bush. He replied, "Over here we can create any kind of bush we want. When we create things by the power of thought, using astral substance, actual materialization occurs. Whatever we create remains as objective reality as long as we wish it to.

"I have told you that on numerous occasions I have been permitted to visit the higher planes. We do function differently there, but I will give you more information on those levels of consciousness at a later date."

Bodily Materialization from the Higher Realms to Lower Realms

Materializations of discarnate persons have been reported in scientific, parapsychological studies, and in some instances such materializations have been photographed. AD told us that, through the power of thought, discarnate persons materialize themselves on earth by using the etheric matter of the earth's atmosphere to make themselves visible to people who ordinarily are not clairvoyant. However, this takes a great deal of thought power, and therefore materializations of this kind do not occur frequently.[20]

---

[20]Such materializations of C. S. Lewis, after his death, are reported in J. B. Phillips, *The Ring of Truth* (New York: Macmillan, 1976), pp. 117-19.

As stated in chapter 7, p. 44, AD told us that the principle of materialization applies even to planes which are higher in frequency of vibration than the astral plane. When people are at a point where they are ready to function more permanently on the higher planes, the astral body is cast off, as in physical death, and they then function in a body compatible with the higher plane.

Concerning materialization on these higher planes, AD said, "When people have passed from the astral plane, they can again come back to it. Through the power of thought, they reclothe themselves in astral substance." He specifically mentioned two well-known persons who have cast off their astral bodies and are now on the mental plane. However, they still manifest themselves on the astral plane by using astral substance to materialize themselves. These two persons are Francis Bacon and Martin Luther. AD stated, "Although these men are on the mental plane, they can return to the astral plane and walk among us and talk with us here."

Multiple and Simultaneous Contact through the Power of Thought

"Through the power of thought, there is an actual *personal* exchange of power between those on earth and those of us in the spiritual world. When you think of me, that thought runs along a pulsating line of force and creates an exchange between us. It is difficult to describe, but I feel it coming like a little golden bead of light. Suddenly I feel it with me, and then I can send a thought to you and it goes back down this little tunnel or thread of light. I know, from a little feeling of impact I get, when it has reached you. Here we can have hundreds and hundreds of these threads of exchanges with different people, and it can be going on all the time."

10
The Power of Prayer

> The prayer of a righteous man has great power in its effects. (James 5:16)

The power of prayer and its importance to life on earth and in the world beyond was emphasized by AD on many occasions. He stated:

"Your praying goes out from you in waves. Nothing is ever lost. When one's thinking is projected, that thinking joins the thinking of other people who are thinking the same way. It may be from a man in Greenland or a man at the South Pole or a man in the tropics. Like attracts like. Such thought becomes a mighty searchlight beam, and *force* is there. You must know, through faith, that this force *is* there, *is* being used, and *is* being directed. Each individual who prays is one of a vast army of people who have these 'searchlights.' In the beginning the beam may be but a tiny flicker, but by faith you can nurture it and know that it is joined in a tremendous band of light which is going around the earth and is being directed. There are multitudinous souls here in the spiritual world who work on these lights. They are attracted toward them and direct the power from them.

"If you could stand back and look at the world, as I have been privileged to do since I've come over here, you would see the flashing of the stars across the sky, the moving of the constellations in space, and threading in among these is this light power of prayer being directed.

"The field of prayer is so wide. There are so many ways to pray and so many reasons to pray. And for every reason to pray, and for every situation which needs to be prayed over, there is an arc of prayer color. Prayer reaches up to us like perfume, like incense—joyously or sadly, pitifully or pleadingly. In many, many different ways, prayer comes up.

"Some people think they don't know how to pray. However, if they but say, 'I do need some help!' and say it with the whole of themselves, unwittingly they have issued a prayer. And it is these prayers that come as feeling from the heart that are the ones that come through the strongest and the most vibrant.

"Repetition in prayer is vain. Prayer that goes on and on and on is like a child nagging at its parent. How can a prayer be answered if you keep on sending out and broadcasting and reiterating and reiterating? Once you have prayed, there must be silence. You must abide in quietness for the answer to come. If you must go about your daily business, do so with an open heart and mind so that your prayer may be answered through an act or a word or a deed or a thought or a hymn or in some other way. It is important for us to remember that we should ask in all sincerity and then say, 'Thank you' and know that the prayer will be answered. A prayer is always answered. Perhaps not always immediately and frequently not in the way that we think it should be, but answered it is. It is never bypassed or allowed to go into oblivion."

An Instructional Trip

On January 17, 1972, AD related, "I had an experience of being over the top of a city the other day. I had been taken on an instructional trip to see how I could negotiate going to another country over different types of terrain, because the vibrations from forest regions are different from the vibrations in the atmosphere over mountains, valleys, plains, the sea, or cities.

"As we came over some villages there was a feeling of light buoyancy, but as we came over one particular city it was like swimming through a sewer. (I've never been in a sewer, but it was what I would imagine a sewer is like—dark and smelly.) Here and there in this city, though, we had an experience of some light, fragrant places. Questioningly I turned to my guide, and he said, 'The fragrant places are associated with a church, chapel, or meeting place where there has been prayer. Some of them are also associated with places like hospitals where there is a selfless giving and a compassionate helping.'

"My guide suggested that I take a look and find where some of the darker places were, and to my surprise many were coming from small groups of houses, places of business, and some schools. In these places there were rebellion, disillusionment, and anger. From these areas rose visual colors that were gray and heavy, and anger produced a fiery red.

"From the churches, or from small groups where there was meditation and prayer, and from some houses where there was a feeling of love, the colors which rose were blue and violet. These colors seemed to be ringed with a glow of golden light.

"Know that when you sit for meditation and for prayer, that goes out into the ether. It will be picked up by your next-door neighbors, others farther away, and also by those unseen ones passing overhead."

Reciprocal Prayers between the Seen and the Unseen

"People have asked, 'What effect do the prayers on earth have on the people who have passed over? Do they help them?' Yes, they do.

"When you, on earth, are joyous and are sending the light,

there is a luminosity that is present in your aura which attracts toward you those from the unseen realms who are feeling in need of such light. They are helped and uplifted. In the same way, when you, on earth, are feeling depressed, those in the unseen realms who are joyous and are sending light can make a link with you and can help to lift you.

"We have our mountaintops and our valleys here, too. We can still feel negative or depressed at times. When I have become depressed over something and I've come down to be near some of my family or some of my friends, I know that I have left them with a depressed feeling. For instance, sometimes you may wake up and feel quite buoyant and good, but in no time at all you may suddenly feel quite flat, and think, 'What's the matter with me?' If that happens, I want you to stop saying, 'What's the matter with me?' Instead, say, 'Now what have I picked up?' Your answer is to pray—to pray that whoever has been near you and is in need of uplifting may receive it. Then visualize the light and send it out.

"You can also get a sudden negative feeling because someone on earth has thought of you and is in need of your help. You can actually pick up this thought by telepathy and begin to feel flat. Later in the day the phone may ring and you may sympathize with the person and talk with him about the problem. However, you are unlikely to link that with your negative feeling earlier in the day unless you actually say, 'Were you thinking about me about 10 o'clock this morning?' If the person says 'Yes,' then you will know why you suddenly had a depressed feeling.

"Whenever you get a sudden negative feeling, you should sit down and pray about it. This will lift you, and it will lift those from the unseen realms, or those on earth, who are linking with you for help. This is *living what you know*. It is a discipline that will pay dividends when you come over here because you will already have done it."

Regular Prayer or Meditation Groups Joined by the Unseen

"When you have regular meditation or prayer groups, there are certain of us from the unseen realms who keep that regular appointment with you. We come to assist you. When you start to pray, we receive and pass on and act as boosters or assistants in your praying. Our power and your power together become more tangible to you than just yours alone. Each prayer group has its own guardians and helpers from the unseen realm. These guardians and helpers, in turn, receive power from you.

"When you pray, you make a beam of light like a funnel of light going up. It becomes dispersed, and then back down the channel you have created come the power and the love and the light given from God. Having received this, you feel warm, you feel light, you feel uplifted, and you say, 'Thank you.' You go your ways and you take that power and light with you. Not only do you keep it for yourself to use but you give it to those you meet and to those who are near to you. They will feel better because they have been with you.

"It is really a bounden duty of those on earth who know anything at all about the power of the Holy Spirit to be emanating that power continuously. The perfect idea, of course, is that one should never need to come together for prayer with anyone else. One should always know that the power of the Holy Spirit is there, receive it, say 'thank you' for it, and know that the grace is with you. That is not easy. You have to be about the business of earning a living and taking care of all the necessities of life that are so important while you are linked with your physical body. However, all of these can and should be transformed through the communication of the inner light which is within you and the outer you which is concerned with the business of everyday living.

"Through regular meditation or prayer groups, and through vital corporate worship, you can receive strengthening and reinforcement from others, both seen and unseen. This corporate power can help you maintain the proper orientation of the inner light within you to the outer you. This can give you a sense of peace and balance in the midst of the turmoil of the world's activities."

Prayer Convocations of the Unseen

"We often have great convocations of souls who assemble here to have pinpointed downpourings of prayer on certain groups, on certain races, or on certain nations of the earth. We have these downpourings for all different people and for all different races at different times, depending on the need.

"Sometimes when we have these downpourings of prayer it is possible for us to see communities that are so shut in on themselves that the power just bounces back. There is a saying that constant dripping wears away a stone, so we continue to pray for them, but it takes a lot of praying to wear away some of those stones.

"There are always groups of people from here praying for their own countries, but sometimes it is necessary that people from all groups here join together to focus on one specific nation.

"When you meditate and when you pray, you should link in with these downpourings of power for the nations of the world. Feel that you are receiving this downpouring, re-channeling it, and sending it out, because, as I've said, our power and your power, functioning together, are stronger than either functioning alone.

"Whenever a world day of prayer is held on earth, there is also great preparation for that day in the spiritual world and large convocations of the unseen join with those on earth in this great prayer experience."

11
Forgive Us Our Sins

> If we say we have no sin, we deceive ourselves, and the truth is not in us. If we confess our sins, he is faithful and just, and will forgive our sins and cleanse us from all unrighteousness. If we say we have not sinned, we make him a liar, and his word is not in us. (1 John 1:8-10)

When he was on earth, AD constantly stressed the importance of the forgiveness of sins. This he continues to emphasize from beyond. He stated, "Guilt feelings resulting from sin produce a weblike thought form which impinges on a person, retarding his growth. On the astral plane these webs can be seen as they are removed through forgiveness.

"If you consider some wrong you feel you have done, you may grieve over it. Circumstances may be such that you cannot directly make amends with the person you have offended. Instead of feeling guilty about it, bring it out and take a look at it in your meditation. Say to yourself, 'Well, I can't do anything about that now because the time has passed, but I will pray never to repeat that again against anybody else. I will now, in my thinking, go back to the person I have offended. I will ask to be forgiven and ask that the incident be forgotten. I will approach that person, soul to soul, in my thinking, in my meditation.' Know that, through the power of prayer and meditation, you actually have made amends with the person you had offended. In a short while you will feel the relief that comes. This web of guilt will actually be taken away from you. It will go. Therefore, it is very foolish to hold onto guilt. It retards you and holds you back and sometimes even brings on actual illness.

"You know, there is a lot to be said for the confession of the Catholics. However, a Catholic, or any other person, can go and confess and may be absolved, but that doesn't prevent some of them from still harboring the thought and retaining a guilt complex.

"There are some people who have a marvelous capacity for receiving absolution and feeling that everything is clear, but they are the blessed ones. They don't have to be Catholic for that, either, because if one truly prays, asks for absolution, lays the whole matter at the feet of the Lord, as they would say in evangelical circles, and then waits to receive the downpouring of power and light which can be received, one can feel truly cleansed. This aspect of forgiveness and the washing away of guilt is taught in many creeds but is not practiced as much as it should be."

Retrospective Pondering

"When people step out of the physical body, they ponder over their lives as a sort of self-judgment. They go back in retrospect, and this pondering weaves itself into a web. If they are bothered by feelings that they have transgressed, they must eventually come to the realization that all can be forgiven and wiped out. In my own life I had made some mistakes which I regretted and which I held in my mind for a while. When I suddenly realized that holding onto guilt feelings wasn't doing me any good whatsoever, it was as though a wind came and absorbed this web of regrets. As I watched, it disappeared into nothing.

"The web of guilt stays with some people a long time on the astral. However, many others work through it within three, four, or five days of death, and they come forth like shining souls without it. People who have pondered over their lives in their old age or during a long illness, before death, are steps ahead. They do not have to go through as much retrospection to shed their web of guilt after they pass over to the astral world."

The Sin of Dogmatism

"Many people, when they come to the astral world, experience a great deal of turmoil and distress because they have been too positive and too dogmatic in their earthly lives and have tried to impose that dogmatism on other people. I think you can find, if you will think about it and look back at your own lives, that there are times when you wish you hadn't been so forceful in persuading someone to do something. When one does this he is cutting across a divinely given attribute of each person, which is free will.

"Dogmatic people who always 'tell you the truth' are very uncomfortable people. They don't understand how uncomfortable they are. When you watch it from here, you see the body blow that 'truth' can be to people sometimes. If something is said too bluntly to a sensitive person who is seeking to improve himself, it can be such a damaging blow that he can retreat and give up.

"People who go around 'telling the truth' and bluntly dogmatizing on what they believe have fewer converts than they think they should have. They mistakenly believe that putting energy and force into what they say will produce converts. Actually, more converts come from demonstrating the law than ever come by dictating the law. This is something worth pondering about."

The Sin of Procrastination

"The sin of procrastination—putting off until tomorrow—is also a source of pain. Life is tenuous. Due to death, tomorrow may never come. Because of things they should have accomplished on earth, but did not, many people are likely to start their astral existence with a sense of incompletion.

"I think it would be wise for people on earth to analyze how they are using their time *each day*. Often they set up a routine which they feel cannot be disturbed. A neighbor may need their assistance at a specific time, but because they are trying to hold strictly to a set routine of their own they may fail to give that help. Things that they have felt were more important often are not, and they may later deeply regret the fact that they neglected to give help when it was needed.

"Procrastination is a fault in character, but it is one of those we tolerate. We say, 'Well, I can put off helping them. There will be plenty of time tomorrow.' However, suppose that someone has been very eager to see you. Tomorrow may be just too late. Someone may not need the help you can give tomorrow, or he may have done something in the meantime that is a wrong course of action, because you didn't see him. He may have known twenty-four hours of loneliness or anxiety that he need not have felt if you had helped him at once.

"There is a story about a fourth wise man who didn't arrive to pay homage to Jesus along with the other three because he had been delayed on the way by helping those in need. I believe, in the eyes of posterity, the fourth wise man would be far more useful than the three who got there.

"Never worry about taking time off to help someone."

Sins of Omission

"Something you should know is that, when we pass over to the astral world and review our life, we grieve more over the sins of omission than the sins of commission.

"For example, there is an artist over here who painted an extraordinary picture while he was on earth. It was a picture of

Jesus on the cross emphasizing, 'Come unto me, all ye that are burdened and heavy-laden, and I will give you rest.' The artist painted the picture because he had felt heavy-laden and had sought and found tremendous relief in this figure on the cross. One day he came in, looked at the picture, and decided he didn't want people to know that he had experienced doubts and had found relief and understanding through Jesus Christ. He took a knife, slashed the picture, and burned it. He then went about his business of doing portraits and commissions. Now that he is over here, the one thing that troubles him is the fact that he did not have the courage to be true to that self of his which painted the picture he destroyed, or the courage to tell people how the door to relief and understanding had been opened to him through Jesus Christ.

"I think there are many people who are going to arrive over here with that same feeling of exasperation, hurt, and rejection. Sins of omission on earth are much more difficult to balance, when you are dead, than sins of commission. This is an extraordinary thing when you think about it.

"And we still have sins of omission here! You must know countless people who start things and then push them in a drawer and forget them. It doesn't stop when you are over here. We start things, but they stay there—hanging in air—until we finish them. And we knock against them, these thoughts. Here sins of omission hit you with a clang, and everyone else can hear that particular note and know that you are slipping again.

"When any individual, on earth or here, omits doing something that he feels and knows he should do, the whole creation feels that loss. Whereas when we do something that adds grandeur and stature to life, the whole created universe gains from that action. It can make you shiver inside to know and appreciate how far-reaching a thought or deed or word of any person can be.

"Thoughts that are not kind ones go around like big, heavy,

sluggish pieces of material—like mud or oil slicks. Thoughts that radiate love, truth, compassion, and understanding leave a glow within us and around us and act like a force to remove the thought forms which are not constructive."

Conscience Is Retained

"The inner voice of conscience is still with us here. I had a feeling that, when I stepped out of my physical body, my conscience would be *me,* but it isn't. It is still a separate part of me which cautions and guides me.

"What we are trying to do, and what you are trying to do, is to become balanced on all levels—to become *whole* persons endeavoring to learn from mistakes made and from right actions done and to build all this into a unified whole. This is a continuing process."

12
Pictures from the Realm Beyond

> All thy works shall give thanks to
> thee, O Lord,
> and all thy saints shall bless thee!
> They shall speak of the glory of thy
> kingdom....
> Thy kingdom is an everlasting kingdom,
> and thy dominion endures
> throughout all generations.
> (Ps. 145:10-13)

Throughout the sittings we were given glimpses of what the astral world is like. We would like to convey some of these to the reader.

In the second sitting with AD, on March 6, 1971, he "retired" for a while and my mother came and spoke with us. Among other things, she described a bit of what the astral world was like. As she was talking, Margaret received a clairvoyant "picture" of my mother walking around a lake.

My mother began, "AD has gone off to 'refresh' himself. I don't know what he calls refreshment, but I'll tell you what my refreshment is. It is walking around our lake and watching the fish jump. We have a beautiful lake here. It is a lovely sky blue color. At the moment the weeping willows are out and downhanging, and the flowers are so beautiful. We have spring over here at the moment. You really do appreciate, don't you, that we think the seasons as they go?

"I have just had a beautiful walk and have thoroughly enjoyed it. I went by myself for a change. Now and then there are times when I really need to go and walk around by myself. People don't crowd in on you here, but their thoughts do. However, when they see you walk off on your own, and you put your protective shield around yourself, you can be very much alone.

"This morning there was the most beautiful music—such an uplifting experience. It was not organ music. It was choirs—an uplifting of great joyousness and happiness. Sometimes I wish that I could communicate it and bring it to you people on earth. I can't compose music. I can't even play anything, but my heart can sing with it. It is not singing with your mouth. It's singing with your whole self—a vibrating joyousness that is quite inexplicable. If you had such an experience in the physical body, you would call it an ecstasy. Here it can be yours all the time, if you wish. There are times when one is bound to get a little nearer the earth, to try to communicate this. However, it gets just a little dulled—like a mirror that gets slightly tarnished with dampness or a silver dish that gets tarnished. That's how you feel, yourself, when you come near the earth—as if the shining you has become just a little tarnished. Now with that poetry, I'm off."

Margaret had received a "picture" while my mother was talking, and she recorded this on the tape. Margaret related:

"In the picture I saw while she was talking, I could see the lake. The lake was quite a large one. I should think it would take about an hour to go around it. It didn't have a path. There was grass down to the edge. There were crocuses and snowdrops and bluebells. Bluebells and crocuses don't grow together in our country, but they do there. She walked through them, and if she stepped on one it sprang up again. It didn't stay bent. She was walking in a blue dress, mid-calf length and sleeveless. It seemed to have embroidery on a sort of boat-shaped neck. The main color that was around her was a deep rose pink. I couldn't see her except as a figure in the distance.

"There were trees. In fact, it looked like a very beautiful picture of Kew Gardens in London, only more so—very well cared for. The grass was about an inch high so that it was just nice to walk on, and it didn't stay flat either. She seemed to be walking in some kind of sandals because her feet seemed flat as she walked around. The aura around her was a pinkish color and it was a protective shield for her.

"I didn't see anyone else. I saw a water fowl on the water and swans, which she stopped to look at. There were also some boulders which people could sit on. At the far end of the lake there was a spring which must have fed the lake. It stirred up ripples on the lake, which was very still...."

My mother must have come back then, for Margaret shifted to the present tense and went on, "She tells me there is an ingress and an exit to this lake. It goes away into a very smooth, quiet-running stream. There are fish in it. I don't see any sun. I see golden light, like sunlight, but I can't see any sun.

"There is music. The air seems to be full of music. Not everybody has to pick it up, though. You only pick up the music if you want to. You don't need to have it if you don't want it. You can shut it out and be in silence.

"She is very slender. Not thin, but slender. I still see the back of her. She looks quite small as if I'm away in the distance looking at her. She is at the far end of the lake now, and she's looking at the spring coming in. There is a little bridge there, rather like a Chinese bridge over the water. It's made of wood and it's lacquered. It's a beautiful green and yellow.

"The whole place appears to be shimmering. You know how, when you look through the heat above a kettle (not the steam part), you see something like a mirage? Well, it is like a mirage. It must be on the higher etheric planes or something like that. It is not on the astral because there is this mirage vibration, and yet it's quite clear in the mirage. It's not often that I get it just like this. Usually it comes flat like a still life, a photograph, or a cinematograph. This seems to be on a different level.

"Now somebody's coming toward her! It's a woman. It's your father's sister. This is what your father says. (He's standing at the back of me now.) He says they are on a different vibration from him—on a different level of consciousness. They're still looking at the water.... Now I've lost them...."

Astral Gardens

On January 26, 1972, AD, being a gardening enthusiast, mentioned the gardens in the realm beyond. He said, "We have beautiful flowers here. The beauty of them and the perfume and the color of them are just indescribable. The strange thing is that when their replicas on earth open only in the evening and at night, they do the same thing here.

"One is not conscious whether there is a sun or no sun. There is simply glorious light.

"We do have a precipitation, a kind of rain which is very pleasant. There is no need for artificial watering of the flowers here. The trees are always at their most perfect. The flowers are always at their most perfect. Nothing dies. As we've said, things are not born over here—they're created.

"I know that many of you will be surprised when I tell you that after a flower reaches its perfection, it can remain like that for a very long time. We create it, bringing it through the bud stage, work it open, and it develops into a perfect flower. When we have kept it as a perfect flower for the length of time we want, we then disintegrate it. We send it out into the ether again so that those particles can be picked up and used again, because nothing is ever lost—nothing is ever wasted. (Even on earth you know that if you've finished with a piece of paper and you burn it, it becomes ash, goes into the air, and is recycled by nature for other uses.)

"I can go and visit one person who has a garden that is completely different from that of another person. We don't have to have gardens here unless we really like them. However, if we are garden enthusiasts, then we go on creating gardens for beauty and for other people to see and enjoy.

"I have a friend here who was a botanist on earth, and he specialized in all varieties of orchids. He collected them from all over the world. He is continuing to work with orchids here, and he has built a most unusual star-shaped glass conservatory. It is composed of about twenty-five pointed sections, and the doorway is on the twenty-sixth. As you come in, you can stand in the middle and look down these radial sections, spreading out like a huge star. It is all glass, clear through. In the center is a sort of three-quarter circle, and in that center part there is a fountain of water which goes up to the glass roof and then sprays down into all these star-shaped sections. The dividers don't reach the roof. They only come up to eye level. When I am in there, I can look over the top of each divider into the next section. These dividers separate the different species of plants. Some are grown from the ground level, and some are on platforms or on shelving, and all the shelving is transparent.

"My friend spends many hours there, and he is crossbreeding, as he calls it. He records his progress with a kind of camera, adding his thought to it, and the picture and words come out on one plate, which he can then project. He is bringing information through, so he tells me, to a number of people in botanical gardens in England, France, and America. There are still two or three gaps in the orchid field on earth. He has them in replica here, but he is waiting for them to be found in their true habitat on earth, which is on a river somewhere off the Andes where white men have not yet been. He hopes that in the next year or so they will be found."

What About Animals That Die?

Any lover of pets knows that they become a true part of a family and are "almost human" in their relationship to the family. In June and August of 1972 we lost two wonderful dogs through death, and we missed them greatly. It was like losing members of the family. We wondered about the survival of dogs as individuals and asked AD about this.

AD stated, "It is perfectly true that all the dogs that we've had in our family I can find here—all of them. They are still individualized. However, the dogs that I knew when I was a boy are no longer here. When I asked why, I was told that they have gone back to the group soul and have added their quota of affection, love, and devotion, to be used again when other dogs come to earth."

Concerning our two dogs he said, "Vicki and Molly are both together. They both are often in your garden, and they both come into the house. They are still very close to the earth because you still think about them, talk about them, grieve over them, in a sense, and love them. This draws them back. They remain for quite some time in the identity that you knew them.

"It is an interesting thing that dogs and cats here come to help their brethren who have been frightened, hurt, or tortured before death. Dogs, such as your Vicki or Molly, that have been secure, help the animals that are not."

Astral Birds and Insects

"I just spent some time up on my lake looking at the water fowl. Two little chicks were pecking at each other. I thought, 'A true family!' I watched them and enjoyed them.

"I don't see many insects here. I've watched honeybees, and I've watched the dragonflies with their beautiful bodies, and some flies. I think I must turn my attention to look at insects for a little while. They are tiny things, and unless one lands on you and you fight it because it has bitten you, you don't really watch them too much. I can't help thinking, 'In my Father's house are many rooms. There are even rooms and areas for the birds and insects.'"

13
Astral Libraries

> Thou dost show me the path of life;
> in thy presence there is fullness
> of joy,
> in thy right hand are pleasures
> for evermore. (Ps. 16:11)

A dear friend of ours, and of AD's, died in April 1969. An outstanding attorney by profession, he was a Jew and an avid student of all theologies. His theological library was the envy of many professional theologians. When he died, the rabbi who officiated at his funeral service quoted a section from the Talmud:

> Jewish folklore tells that not only are there houses of study here on earth, but that God, Himself, has a Yeshiva Shel Maalah—an Academy on High. Moses studies there, and Hillel and Rabbi Akiba—and whenever a scholar dies, a place is waiting for him in the Yeshiva Shel Maalah.

The picture of our friend, busily studying in the Yeshiva Shel Maalah, was one that I could not get out of my mind. Probing the truth in his theological books was one of the most absorbing interests in his life. The logic of his continuing to do this in the realm beyond rang true.

A place in the libraries of God would certainly also be reserved for AD, who always had an intense desire to "be with the great minds of the ages" through books.

As mentioned in chap. 7, p. 44, AD stated that those who were avid students of the written word on earth still felt impelled to visit libraries and reading rooms on the astral plane. This intrigued us, and we questioned him about it in later sittings.

On October 5, 1972, AD came prepared to tell us about astral books, libraries, and research rooms. He stated:

"When we first come to the astral plane, we can study in libraries which are very much like the libraries we have on earth. It is very important that these should be here, for if one were transported after death into completely new surroundings, the sense of continuity would be broken. I want to stress again that the astral world is almost a replica of your world, except that it is of a finer substance. Therefore, as we have pointed out before, on the astral plane we continue to practice many of the modes of living we carried out on earth.

"We have books that would seem to be exactly like the books on earth. As long as we think that we need books, we may go to a library, look through the catalogues in the stands, go to the shelves, and find the correct book. There are librarians here, still doing the same kind of work. We also have museums and art galleries here which contain replicas of the great art of the ages, and some people still find a need to study in those places.

"However, the time comes when you no longer want to go around in a regular library and get your information in this way. Your own thinking and your own progress give you a desire to get information a quicker way. We can then go to memory-bank reference libraries, which contain records of everything that has ever happened.

"For instance, I sat in on a meeting of a committee on malnutrition of the United Nations on earth, and I was wondering what had led up to this particular meeting and what had gone on before. Consequently, I applied to see the memory banks of the previous meetings of this committee.

"The memory-bank reference library to which I went was a long, low building in the middle of a parklike area. Between some pillars at the front of the building I found the list of subjects which could be studied in this particular reference library. I found, properly indexed, the number of the room in which I could study the proceedings of the past meetings of the United Nations committee in which I was interested.

"I proceeded down a very beautiful long corridor with green and blue carpeting, as if I were going down the corridor of a museum or art gallery. Light came into the corridor from skylights in the roof.

"When I came to the proper room, I knocked on the door and a voice said, 'Come in.' I went in and found a middle-aged man who looked like a Pakistani. He was impeccably dressed in gray tunic and trousers. His name was Mr. Asaf. We shook hands and he motioned me to a seat. I outlined what I wanted, using my notes concerning this committee which was dealing with malnutrition. I told Mr. Asaf that I wanted to find out more about where the main malnutrition problems were, and what local crops and resources were in those problem areas of the world.

"He ushered me to a very comfortable chair to which earphones were connected. This chair had very broad arms with control knobs on them. Mr. Asaf had me swivel the chair around to better view a screen that was in the room, on which visual information would be projected. The knobs on the chair controlled the visual information projected to this screen and also controlled the sound commentaries which came through the earphones to accompany the visual picture. Through these controls, I could also make a duplicate recording of all of it, if I wished, so that I could take away the information and replay it later. This was really a matter of automatically collecting information which could be used later.

"When I pressed one button, charts of statistics were

projected on a visual screen. I found they were too far ahead of the sound channel, and it took me a little while to get it adjusted. I later realized that across the room there were lights flashing on certain cabinet doors. By going over there and by opening the doors that were flickering with light, I also found that I could lift from these cupboards sheets of paper on which the information was printed by some automatic process. Therefore, there were three ways in which I could rapidly secure information in the memory-bank reference libraries. I could see it on a screen, I could hear explanatory comments, and I could have it recorded in written form for later reading. As I mentioned before, the visual and sound portions could also be recorded for later use.

"It's scarcely true to say that the way material is displayed here is like the computers in your denser world, but I guess it is on the same principle. As I was not too knowledgeable of how computers worked on earth, neither am I too sure of how this works. If I were inquisitive I could find out and tell you, but the results are what I always look for. The working principles of these things I leave to those who are specialists in these areas. When I was on earth, the only concern I had about computers was that we should be careful that man did not become their slaves, instead of computers being servants for men."

14
Occupations in the Realm Beyond

> We know that in everything God works for good with those who love him, who are called according to his purpose. (Rom. 8:28)

AD has pointed out that he is trying to give a clear picture of the conditions he is encountering, from his own perspective. Therefore, we cannot expect a complete overview of all occupations and activities which occur in the spiritual world. However, AD does give some indications of the wide scope of these.

In one of the first sittings AD told of traveling all over the world with a friend who had died shortly before he did. AD said, "We have been traveling extensively and have even been to take a look at the troubles in Ireland. Soon we must settle down and make up our minds what our work is to be. A job is not simply allocated to you here. As there is choice of occupation on earth, so there is even greater choice of occupation in what you may like to call 'heaven.' I find the latitude in our choices here to be quite incredible. I don't know what field I will enter at the present time. I will have to pray over this and inquire into various fields, because once we are committed, we are committed for a considerable time. Here we don't work so much as individuals. We work more in bands and groups."

We were told that persons sometimes continue using skills they had on earth. Others train for entirely different occupations, depending on their own aptitudes and desires. Many of the occupations seem to be service-oriented or research-oriented. AD specifically mentioned doctors, nurses, botanists, librarians, teachers, ministers, musicians, and artists.

In one session AD told us that all is not work in the spiritual realms. There are periods for relaxation and play there, too, and particularly for the young people, who enjoy many of the activities they knew on earth.

15
AD Meets Some Theologians

> Therefore are they before the
> throne of God,
> and serve him day and night
> within his temple;
> and he who sits upon the throne
> will shelter them with his presence.
> (Rev. 7:15)

Having been a theologian, AD quite naturally would have some contacts with theologians there. Among others, he specifically mentioned James A. Pike, Pierre Teilhard de Chardin, Charles Wesley, John Knox, and Martin Luther.

AD said, "Ruth, you will be interested to know that I have met Bishop Pike. Bishop Pike has been badly misunderstood. He is very sincere and a very kind-hearted and generous man. He has been extremely helpful to me. I have had several conversations with him. He has placed himself at the disposal of the 'elders' over here to help those who come over as ministers from whatever church. Bishop Pike is no longer a bishop, of course. Over here we don't use titles. He is particularly dedicated in trying to help some of the more dogmatic 'dyed-in-the-blood' theologians who come over. God help the man! He's got a job."

Margaret had received a "picture" of AD's reception when he first passed over. He called it "at home" day. She described in detail the people she saw greeting him, including in particular a man who wore a flat hat with a round brim such as the French priests wear. AD had been deeply interested in Pierre Teilhard de Chardin and his work, and we asked him if this was Father Teilhard whom Margaret saw.

AD said, "Yes, it was he. He welcomed me and he told me that all who think about him and reach out toward him are under his special benediction and blessing. However, our paths are not merging or running side by side. Teilhard is concerned now in substantiating the truth that he brought through. It seems to me that he is concentrating on the brethren of his own Jesuit order."

In another sitting AD told us that he had had the privilege of hearing Charles Wesley preach. He stated, "Charles Wesley is one of the many teachers and sages who, of their own volition, are staying near the earth to work with people when they first come over. These sages are dedicated to help certain people go through stages that these persons never faced or had the opportunity to go through in the physical body."

On another occasion AD mentioned meeting John Knox: "I understand that John Knox did come now and again and add his quota of push to me when I was a younger man on earth, and particularly when I was working for the rights of the underprivileged. He is an unusual little man. When he wants to get something across to me, he punctuates everything he says with a blow from one hand into the palm of the other. He thinks that because I am an American I don't understand his Scottish accent. He has been over here a long while and he could very easily communicate by thought instead of speech, but he enjoys talking."

Before one sitting, Margaret and I were talking about Swedenborg's image of Martin Luther as a person who was very frustrated in the realm beyond—frustrated by the fact that Lutherans on earth were using only a portion of his understanding.

AD disagreed with this. He stated, "I know what

Swedenborg said about Luther, but I don't find him a 'frustrated' person.

"I have twice been in contact with Luther, once when he spoke at a convocation of about 20,000 Lutherans who had gathered together. There he implied that Lutheran teaching as it is at present should be widened and expanded. As man's understanding of scientific things has expanded, man's understanding of religious things has not expanded to the same extent. Luther felt there should be a downpouring of power from the Lutherans who have passed over upon the Lutherans who are incarnate. He expressed a desire for an expansion of consciousness, for barriers to be knocked down and more ground to be taken in. For example, Luther feels that there should be an intensification of such things as the laying on of hands. This is tentatively used at the present time, but not forcefully. If the pastors who are using the laying on of hands would open themselves more widely, there could be tongues of fire of healing instead of 'candle flames.'

"If you will reread some of the principal first teachings of Martin Luther and look at them with the eyes of the Spirit, you will see that all you are exploring and understanding today is hinted at there. It is there, but it would have been out of time for him to preach then what he is sending down to his people now. If he had preached and taught that at the time he was on earth, people would not have listened to him. Remember that he was preaching and teaching to a certain nationality of people—people who had disciplined and rigid ideas. Their very climate kept them rigid and disciplined. Within the confines of the disciplined body they had, and the disciplined political and national structure, he was showing them how to break down some of the barriers. If he came back now, it would be the same teaching but it would be translated on different levels and in different ways. Everything grows—everything.

"Although Luther feels there should be a new growth of

consciousness in the Lutheran church, I do not find him 'frustrated' over any hedges that have been built. Instead, I find him to be a most tolerant mind and very understanding, but still fiery. He is far beyond what I had conceived from his writings. I find him still an electrifying force, a great awakener. He is a great soul. When I think of him, and when I think of the work he did, then it overwhelms me with my inadequacy and the inadequacy of all of us to translate the tremendous thoughts that he brought.''

16
No Measured Time

> . . . with the Lord one day is as a thousand years, and a thousand years as one day. (2 Pet. 3:8)

There is much that we cannot comprehend concerning the freedom from the bounds of time in the spiritual world.

It is evident to us that AD is still conscious of our divisions of time on earth. He often will refer to "yesterday morning," or "about last August in your time," and so on. Yet he states, "We don't talk about time here. We talk about opportunity. We cannot think about time here because it is not measured off in days and nights and months and years."

This evidently has its effect on the discipline of life in the astral world, as AD commented at one sitting:

"I want to put on record that I find life here more interesting than one could dream possible, but it does detract from quiet thinking periods. I am slowly realizing that there is a greater need for self-discipline than when a physical body made its demands known. Then I had time divided up into sleep and waking, and the latter part divided into eating, talking, studying, teaching, walking, thinking, etc. Here there is so much to see, so much to hear, so much to do. One has to learn to set aside some 'time' for one's own personal self-discipline, because if the mind doesn't control the body you can be in the same state of utter discord as you are when you are in the physical body. Discipline brings order, and it is absolutely imperative to have orderliness."

According to AD, completely extended vision is not an automatic attribute gained when man enters the spiritual world. He states, "Here there is an overall awareness of what is going to happen on earth six weeks, six months, or perhaps two years ahead. At times it is rather like being in an airplane looking down, and we get an overview or prevision of what is going to happen, due to our being able to see things in a broader perspective. However, do not for one moment imagine that, now that we are here, we automatically have completely extended vision and have become seers. That is not true. However, we do have some who are seers here. They are souls who, through much trial, tribulation, and service, have been permitted to see in a more extended way. It is not something that just happens to you automatically. Anyone can make a calculated judgment on a thing, but to be a seer—to be a prophet like the Old Testament prophets—means that there has been great endeavor. There has been testing and the development of certain faculties, which are more prominent in that person who is the seer than in those of us who are not."

There is indication that precognition[21] and postcognition[22] still happen to people in the spiritual world, as they do to some people on earth. There have been many reports in parapsychological literature concerning such experiences of people on earth. On the basis of his studies, Dr. Lawrence LeShan

---

[21] An experience of something that will happen in the future on the time continuum.

[22] An experience of something that already has happened in the past on the time continuum.

points out that these experiences usually occur spontaneously, without being willed.[23]

AD related an interesting postcognitive experience that he had had in the spiritual world. He said, "I went to do some research on the records of a conference which was held in England concerning unification of the churches there. While I looked at the memory banks of the past on a screen and heard the sound recording, as I had done in the research libraries before, I suddenly found myself actually in the midst of this conference with two of the men who were discussing the possibilities of such a unification. This was a strange experience. It was as if I had been watching a television screen where you see things on videotape that have happened in the past. Suddenly I found myself in the middle of it. I was actually standing there, and there were people and I could touch them. I knew that by some alchemy of thinking I was suddenly with them and I could converse with them."

Man has much to learn about the interrelationships of time, or the absence of time, as we know it. Perhaps in future sittings with AD we may glean more insight into this area. Right now, all we can state is that we know that precognitive and postcognitive experiences occur, but we do not yet understand why they occur and how they occur.

In his introduction to the parapsychological monograph by Lawrence LeShan, Henry Margenau of Yale University states:

> I believe that in a universal sense which is above time, all events are present and real *now*. Perhaps all future and past existence is uniquely on record, conserved in an eternal reservoir of happenings, firmly engraved in timeless essence or, as some

---

[23]Lawrence LeShan, *Toward a General Theory of the Paranormal* (New York: Parapsychology Foundation, 1969), pp. 93-95.

would say, in the mind of a universal consciousness. To apprehend the "S-IR"[24] we move through the all, seeing it through a slit-like window which moves along the axis of time. Perhaps the mystic has no window and is exposed indiscriminately to the universal record of the all, or, to use Whitehead's phrase, to the treasure house of God's universal memory.[25]

---

[24]Sensory Individual Reality, a term used by Dr. LeShan in his monograph to denote common-sense individual reality as perceived by man through the senses.
[25]From Henry Margenau's introduction to the parapsychological monograph by LeShan, *Toward a General Theory of the Paranormal,* used by special permission of the Parapsychology Foundation, Inc.

17
Personal Responsibility—Universal Responsibility

> Bear one another's burdens, and so fulfil the law of Christ. (Gal. 6:2)

While on earth, AD once wrote:

> Justice is one virtue which must never be separated from love. Only that love is true love which is just. No form of injustice can be reconciled with Christian love, no matter how much sentimentality there may be in that love. The Christian professing to have love for his fellow man while tolerating injustice being done to him does not have Christian love. If he would but realize that justice is an aspect of love, many caricatures of Christian love would be avoided.[26]

AD constantly stressed our responsibility to our fellow man and the fact that we are our brother's keeper. This he continues to stress:

[26] A. D. Mattson, *Christian Ethics* (Rock Island, Ill.: Augustana Book Concern, 1947), p. 204.

"Every man is responsible for himself, but because all men are brothers and sisters and all are children of God, they are also his responsibility. This responsibility lies fairly and squarely on everybody's shoulders.

"The Bible is a massive guidebook for everyday living in carrying out our individual and group responsibilities. There is always an interpretation that fits today. It is not a revelation for 1176, or 1872, or 1975, or 2075. It is an everlasting revelation. Every time a Bible is picked up, even if only casually, and opened up to look for guidance, the light and power of God are focused on that person and that Bible."

The Importance of the Now

AD stated, "Many people from backward and underprivileged areas of the world find themselves unable to adapt to life after death when they first pass over. Due to environmental circumstances on earth, they have not had the opportunity to grow and develop, and have often 'vegetated' on earth. The dull, routine type of existence they have had puts them in a frame of mind to stay earthbound after death, near old familiar surroundings where they find a sense of comfort. However, this holds them back from any progress they could make in the spiritual world. We have many working here to try to help these people. When you are praying, send out a thought that power may go to all those who are working to release these backward, earthbound spirits so that they, too, can move forward and on."

Concerning philosophies of life that retard man's growth, AD stated, "The fatalistic philosophies of the many millions of people in the East, in such countries as India, are a retarding factor for man's progress on earth. Fatalists feel that things are going to happen anyway and there is nothing that can be done about it, and so they just relax and accept things as they are. It's the easy way out. They think, 'It really doesn't matter.

When we die, we're going to go on and therefore we do not really have to accept responsibility for the life that is within us, manifested through the physical body in a physical world.' This of course is a negation of life and what it means. Until the millions of people in the East, and in other countries where people have lost all personal initiative, realize this, we can't truly have peace and harmony in the world.

"Man has to think of life everlasting, manifested *now* in the present. This is very important. Life has been held very cheaply. Millions of people have been killed through devastation, torture, war, and man's inhumanity to man. This has brought spiritual pollution on all levels.

"While we are speaking about spiritual pollution, I want to point out another destructive area in man's inhumanity to man—that of man's hate against his brother, expressed in verbal ways. We see from here that a verbal feud can be as devastating to the participants as a shooting feud—sometimes worse. If someone is shot down, it is mainly an attack on the physical body and the inner self is released. This is certainly murder and a heinous crime. However, in a verbal hate feud, the spiritual bodies are attacked, sometimes in a stronger and more damaging way than when a physical body is destroyed by shooting. This is something very important for people to realize."

Interaction of the Realms

"A moral decision that is not right in the physical world can cause a confusion in the spiritual world. In the same way, if we in the spiritual world turn our backs on a situation on earth and say, 'Well, let them be, I have other things I want to do,' we can cause showers of confusion to come there.

"We are just as much morally obligated to help our brothers on earth when we are without a physical body as we were within a physical body. This is an aspect of truth that few people want to face. They think, 'Oh, when I'm dead everything will sort itself out. There will be no troubles, and that will be that.' That is not true. God still gives us the opportunity and responsibility in the spiritual world to observe and to choose and to serve.

"It is not going to be pleasant for a lot of people to know that, whether they like it or not, they are their brother's keeper. We are each other's keeper. We are each other's deterrent. We are each other's goad and help, because we are all part of the ONE pulsating, living, glorious WHOLE.

"I say glorious in spite of the terrible things that are still happening in the world, because man *is* progressing up in the spiral of evolution. From here we know that there is no problem, there is no pain, there is no ill, there is no disharmony in the whole of the created universe that *eventually* will not be made into harmony. This is an awareness that one gets here which is harder to achieve on earth. It is something I want you to try to remember."[27]

Throughout the sittings AD gave many examples of how people in the spiritual world assist people still on earth. Some of those are indicated in other chapters. We shall relate other examples here.

In one of the very first sittings AD told us of the work his father was doing. "My father took me to see the results of the famine and the tidal wave in East Pakistan [now the new nation of Bangladesh]. He seems to have adopted these people as his focal point of serving. He has an uncanny awareness of their abilities and also of their basic tendency to procrastinate as long as they have enough for today. This is not a 'mañana' at all. It is more a putting off further than tomorrow. They have the attitude that 'Someday I'll be in Nirvana so it doesn't really matter what I'm lacking today.' It's a patient dumb-suffering. This is very keenly understood and felt by Father.

---

[27]Concerning man's responsibility in achieving this harmony, we quote from AD on p. 145.

He knows how to deal with it and how to help them. He gets in touch with them and gives them little impressions to make them realize that the sun is high and it's time they got things done. He is not dealing with them when they're dead. He is dealing with those who are still living. He has a fine group of associates with him who work to help them in their sleep. As we've indicated before, while the religions of India were fine in the time when they were conceived and brought through for these people, they don't prepare them very well for today's forward movement, and that whole country is moving forward."

My cousin William Hoag, who died in 1942 after a long and painful cancer illness, had come to visit AD. Bill told AD that his work was varied but mostly involved helping those who had been badly wounded as a result of war. AD said, "Bill helps those war casualties who still have to stay on earth and are not allowed to come over to us yet. This is a very tedious and very special kind of work. These wounded people have to be given the courage and strength to go on living, even though they may be badly crippled.

"Those who work with these disabled people are mostly souls who themselves died after a long period of illness or a painful one. Those who have suffered and tried to live, and then have had to give up the fight and be taken over, know the efforts that have to be made. They are able to help the disabled when they are out of the body during sleep. They help them to have a positive attitude to go forward and fight against the various problems that come with disability.

"I think that we have to have a little different viewpoint toward the physically handicapped people. We must realize that great effort of will has to be used by the handicapped just to function in their physical bodies. Therefore, a greater responsibility is placed upon those on earth who do not have to fight against a personal disability to use their wills and energies in constructive ways to combat social ills."

When he was on earth, AD was always probing the various

social problems facing mankind. He was particularly interested in the hunger problems that plague the earth. In the astral world he continues to have these concerns. He has related how he has been gathering extensive information on hunger problems throughout the world. We were told that information, gathered through studies in the spiritual world, with the overview that they have there, is passed on to people on earth who are concerned with the same areas of study. The people on earth can draw on this information in attempting to work out solutions for the world's problems.

Humanism Is Not Enough

In several sittings AD brought through specific information concerning some people who had died. They had been "social actionists," trying to achieve a better world but without much religious motivation in their well-meaning efforts. We were told that they were finding it very difficult to accept their death and to adjust to the spiritual world in which they found themselves.

Some of AD's statements in his book *Christian Ethics* have a bearing here. In that book he stated:

> Every deed has a cosmic relationship and is thus related to God. . . . Ethics cannot be complete without some attempt to set human conduct and history in their cosmical environment. The weakness of all forms of humanism is that they do not answer the question as to the cosmic place of the moral. Ethics without religion is in the same category as physics without astronomy. The good must be the power that rules the world, or it is difficult to see why I should be under obligation to obey it. Our sense of absolute obligation involves not only that we are striving to attain the moral but also that it is assigned

to us by the World-Ground. Our sense of dependence and our obligation must find a common meeting point. Such a meeting point can be found only in God....

Religion gives to the soul a peace and joy which the moral struggle by itself can never produce. Ethics can never take the place of religion in the great crises of life. It has little comfort to offer in suffering, in bereavement, or in the face of death.[28]

---

[28]Mattson, *Christian Ethics,* pp. 75, 78, 206.

18
Reciprocal Worship between the Seen and the Unseen

> . . . those that were sown upon the good soil are the ones who hear the word and accept it and bear fruit, thirtyfold and sixtyfold and a hundredfold. (Mark 4:20)

On numerous occasions AD spoke about the fact that those from the unseen realms often participate with us in our worship services on earth. He related, "People in the astral realm are often attracted back to their churches on earth, and they find tremendous pleasure in giving color and light and love to the congregation that they have left. They, in turn, receive strength and help from those in that congregation when they are thought of and are remembered and are prayed for. Therefore, prayers for the departed members of a congregation should be a vital part of every worship service.

"When we unseen ones join you in worship, we sit in the pews if there are empty ones. If not, we stand at the back of the church or in the aisles and we observe. From the auric colors around individuals, we can determine those who have received a genuine touch of the Lord and those who have not.

"Since I have eyes no longer clouded by physical eyesight, I have seen *so clearly* the fact that the churches have belied man's trust in them by never truly giving to the last dreg. When the widow was asked to give, she gave of her last mite (Mark

12:42-44). Can we ever feel that the church has given the ultimate? I am not thinking in terms of the vast holdings of some of the churches. I am rather thinking of those who are called to minister, and also those who participate as laymen—have they given the ultimate of themselves in their ministries?

"You've heard sermons that are nicely polished and all put together according to the liturgy for the day, and quoting a book here and there. The minister outlines his sermon. It's an outline all right. It's a skeleton, but what *flesh* has been put on it? And when flesh is put on it, what *breath* has been put in it? This is something I struggled with when I was in a body, and it is something that troubles me now because I am seized more than ever with the realization of the importance of putting *life* into people—illumine the Word, put life into it, put breath into it. There are many of us here, joining together, who stand behind the teachers and preachers of the Word, and we try to help bring through living thought into the words they are giving.

"When you laymen sit in the pews and listen, do you simply say, 'Oh, yes, that was a very nice sermon, very nice,' and then immediately go out and go back to the same old treadmill you were on before? You come to church loaded with problems, and we hope that you're going to lay them at the feet of the Lord. You know you can pray and be absolutely released from them. Then why do you get outside of the church and proceed to take them with you again? If you don't leave your problems behind, how can you feel that, through worship, they are forgiven or gotten rid of or helped?

"The quiet pause that comes at the end of a service should be a time through which you absorb deeply that which you have received in the service. Take it into yourself so that you can hold it firmly, and then you can take it with you through the week. You should go and sit quietly in the car before you drive away and say to yourself, 'May I hold what I have received until I get home, and may I then find a few quiet moments to further absorb it.' This conscious effort will reinforce your worship experience.

"People in the congregation often feel that they come to a service only to receive. They must also realize that what they *give* matters greatly. Their positive participation is very important to the total worship pattern of that congregation.

"I am still a little puzzled and disturbed about the lack of unity in worship. There are congregations that do have a unity, but there are some where you find many people whose threads are still not in the pattern. It seems to me that there should be the warp and the woof that is woven in and out—the weaving in and out of the vibrations of the emotions and the feelings—and a whole gathering up and surging up in the total worship experience. This is difficult sometimes because there are those who, while in the middle of the congregation, are actually out on the fringe. There is nothing coming from them.

"Sometimes I go along with you to your church, Ruth, and I sit by you and I look at the congregation and I see a person thinking, 'Oh, pastor, that's a bit farfetched, isn't it?', and I see a purply green-looking cloud coming up from him. I go over to him and say, 'It's not as farfetched as you think.' And then I feel, 'Well, I haven't gotten through to him.' My guardian who is with me says, 'AD, where's your faith? You've planted a thought in his mind. It's up to him now.'

"But you know it's more difficult to plant thoughts in some people's minds than in others. Some people just haven't got any ground to plant them in. I don't mean they haven't any mind, but their mind is so full of themselves. It's hard to pull the weeds out and find a little spot to plant anything. Have you ever found that? When you meet someone like that you probably think, 'Well, now, how am I going to get a thought or an idea into that person? He is so bigoted and so ego-centered!' My advice to you is to wrap your thought in the love of God and just pitch it at his heart and wait. That is what we do. You know there is a cosmic bloodstream that circulates through the body like the physical bloodstream. It will get up to his head eventually, maybe weeks later, maybe months, maybe years, but it is stored there, and one day it will have its effect.

"On one occasion when I attended your church, there was a lady toward the back, on the righthand side, who was feeling very gray and concerned. She was thinking, 'Such an effort, but I made it to church—so now what?' I watched the way her own relatives from the unseen, her own mother in particular, brought light to her. She wasn't really entering into the service for a while, and then suddenly she became caught up in the corporate worship. When she came out of the church, she said, 'Well, I'm glad I came. I'm glad I made the effort.' She went away with the reward of the effort. One obtains a reward for every effort that one makes. It may not be a seen reward on earth. It may be an unseen reward, breaking down of a barrier in the wholeness of you."

The Reciprocal Effect of Unsaid Thoughts in Worship

Telepathy, or communication by thought, evidently plays its part in worship. AD stated, "An important thing you should know is that unsaid thoughts are transmitted and have their effect during worship.

"Sometimes a pastor will say, 'While I was preaching, there was so much coming in for me to say that I felt I hadn't gotten my message over as well as I wanted.' I want the pastors to know that while they are speaking and giving their sermons, the additional unspoken thoughts that come racing around at the back of their minds are actually being transmitted as well, and someone in the congregation is picking them up. The reaction in the listener may be, 'Well, yes, that's so, but you haven't gone quite as far as you might. You could have said *this* and added a little more.' Pastors shouldn't be concerned that they actually haven't said all they intended, because some in the congregation do pick up the unspoken message. If I had known that when I was teaching on earth, I wouldn't have been so frustrated over not presenting everything I wanted to. I would have realized that some of the thoughts in my mind were going out as well and were being picked up by my students. What I said aloud provoked, but what I was thinking, but not saying, also entered in.

"Also, you laymen in the congregation need to be very careful what kind of thoughts you broadcast back to a pastor. You can adversely affect him and the message he is trying to give if you think to yourself, 'He's not much of a preacher, is he? He hesitates in his delivery and it really is very dull.' We have to remember that delivery is not all-important. We don't know what else his mind is directing and what our minds are picking up. Therefore, we should not condemn, even if we can't praise the way a sermon is given. We can only have faith that this man has been directed to say this to the best of his ability. We cannot set ourselves up as judges as to whether he is giving his best or not—that burden is on the minister himself.

"In spite of what we have said about the necessity for vital preaching, we don't help the situation by having a negative attitude. Even if the message doesn't inspire us, a positive attitude can help us to gain from it. We can listen, and we can develop in our minds what we would have said if we were preaching. Therefore, we *are* actually feeding on what is being given, are adding to our own understanding, and are widening our ideas. If nothing else, it is forcing us to evaluate and to exercise our minds. Then those from the unseen realms can nurture that evaluation in us and can help us to further expand. A positive attitude, therefore, will be fruitful, but a negative attitude will be detrimental, not only to the minister but to the others in the congregation as well.

"Later, if you recall something that was helpful to you from a service, give a personal expression of credit to the minister—a note, a word, a thank you, or a prayer that will reach him. Ministers need this kind of reciprocation. The minister gives. You as a congregation receive. However, the minister also needs to receive from your interest, your thought, your ideas, your vocal thanks, and your prayers.

"Something of which I have become more acutely aware is that a sense of unity in a congregation can be helped by the custom of the pastor greeting the congregation through the shaking of hands after the service. This custom, as a symbol of brotherhood, goes back to the earliest days of religious worship, not only with the worship of the Christian church but in the worship of other temples and groups of people. Through the hand clasp there is a positive current that passes between people which can be a unifying bridge. This personal contact of greeting should be practiced by all who minister. Such personal greeting between a Sunday school teacher and members of the class can also be beneficial. I want to bring an awareness of the importance of this to those who don't practice it."

Ministering Angels—the Wind of the Spirit

"There are teams of invisible ones in the spiritual world who are known as ministering angels or agents of the Holy Spirit. They are attracted to different worship services on earth where their help is needed. I have joined such groups at various times, as has your mother.

"If an individual on earth has been seeking spiritual enlightenment, is on the verge of receiving light, inspiration, and understanding, and would benefit from assistance and help, a call is sounded in the astral realm and we go to help.

"The touch of God may come to that person through a hymn or a prayer or an idea from the minister. It lodges and it grows and is stored to be considered later. One by one we commit ourselves to these individuals needing support to hold onto that enlightenment, and for the next few days we walk with them.

"We know that person has to go out into the world and meet all sorts of distractions and problems. Maybe his car will be hard to start, or a child clutches at him, or he has to visit someone who is ill. There are television and other diversions, and the Sunday passes with multitudinous happenings. Perhaps when he goes to bed he's too tired even to remember what happened in the morning at the service. This, then, is our thrust. We are near him and, when he is out of his physical body in sleep, we remind him of what he experienced in the morning. We help him to go through the experience again, to enlarge on it, to feel it as a sensation, and to know what this enlightenment is eventually going to mean to his total life.

"The process is like a woodsman who takes two sticks and rubs them together and gets a spark. He blows on the spark to make it burst into flame. He feeds the fire with little chips of wood and twigs before it can take a log. Like the woodsman, there are those in the spiritual world who act as the wind of the Spirit which blows and who add fuel to expand the new thought in the mind of a person. They protect and look after the light in that person so that it will grow in him. It may take months, it may take years—or it may take but a few hours.

"This takes place not only in Christian churches but in all churches, wherever there is a downpouring of spiritual power. Wherever there is an awakening or a chance of an awakening, we go to blow the wind of the Spirit on it. You can understand what a fascinating thing this is, but it can also be very tedious. Sometimes you can keep prodding on and on, and nothing will happen for a long time. However, there can be tremendous moments when we can step back and know that the person is firm in his inner peace and that we have succeeded in our efforts.

"Your mother was working with such a group, and she told me about one case in particular. She was in a Roman Catholic church where there was a young girl about nineteen or twenty years old. The girl was very troubled because she was not quite sure whether she should or should not take a path that would bring her marriage to someone not of her faith. Her strong prayer attracted the group of ministering angels in that church, and your mother volunteered to stay with her. After the service your mother had a difficult time because the girl's parents were nagging at the girl about the problem. This nagging was aggravating the conflict within the girl. However, that afternoon your mother was able to engineer it so that the girl took a walk alone.

"Subtly inspired by what she saw of the beauty of nature, the girl began to experience a deepening of the awareness of the 'beat' that is in all living things, that beat which we call the cosmic consciousness—the Christ Force. Unexpectedly, while on this walk, she met the young man. Seeing him in the light of her new awareness, she realized that she was not strong enough to bridge across the differences of their faith. She told him this, and the man took it very badly. Instead of trying to understand, he became very angry and shouted at her. The girl realized that if he could behave this way now, he would surely behave this way after they were married. She then knew the answer to her problem, and so your mother was released.

Worship on the Astral Plane

"On the astral plane we still have great cathedrals and great churches. Ministers who preached on earth, and still feel the urge to do so, continue to preach here. I am one of those continuing to preach.

"It is an interesting thing that over here, as soon as I am finished, I am confronted with an analysis of what I have said. This analysis takes the form of a color chart, reflecting the patterns of auric color engendered by the people of the congregation. The thoughts and reactions of the people to whom I am speaking come up in front of me in the form of great channels of color. These color emanations are recorded on tape to form the color charts. Afterward we may again receive the reactions by viewing the charts to see how much we achieved of what we had intended. The various colors were explained to me. The fact that there was much gold signified that I had touched many heart rays and that these people were uplifted. However, I had spoken in one sermon about forgiveness and I found that this portion of my sermon had not gotten home at all because there was very little reaction to that. When people are touched emotionally, there are blue and green colors of emotional tears—cleansing and helpful. Through study of these charts we learn how to present our thoughts more effectively the next time.

"We also have tremendous prayer meetings here, through which we mutually uplift each other. I had not realized how important worship of this kind would continue to be."

19
Worship Research

> O come, let us worship and bow down,
> let us kneel before the Lord, our Maker!
> For he is our God,
> and we are the people of his pasture,
> and the sheep of his hand.
>
> (Ps. 95:6-7)

On February 27, 1972, AD related, "I looked into your church this morning, and I was happy at the vibrations that I felt there and the colors that were evident. I was joining with a small group of us who are analyzing, as far as it is possible for us to analyze, what we feel about the worship that is coming from various areas of the world today.

"There is a project going on over here to study the intensity of color and power that comes from the church services of the various denominations in various areas of your continent, in Europe, and in Asia. This study is not restricted to worship in Christian churches. We now have four groups working on this project, and I happen to be in a Christian group.

"I did not voluntarily seek this position but was asked to join the group. When I inquired of my guardian why I was asked to join them, I was told that it was because I was passing this information through to you, Ruth. There is not another one of this group who has ever passed through any information, or even *thought* of passing any through. They call me their 'public relations man.'

"I am the only one in our group who is representative of the basic teachings of the Protestant churches. There are six of us in the group I work with, and the leader is one who has been here many centuries. He had been a Druid when on earth. I understand from the information that has been given to me that he was converted to the early Christian teachings and was one of the prime movers in organizing and passing the teaching as it came from Palestine to the more northern places. The Druids were the respository of the ancient mystical teaching of the three in one, as symbolized by their mistletoe, the three berries together. It was a very powerful and very mysterious sect and quite widely spread over northern Europe. This man is filled with white and golden light. He is youngish. He has come back to middle age and he always wears his white robe and nearly always carries his silver sword—his contact with the power. He is very moon-orientated and seems to be most interested in the phases of the moon.

"We have another man in the group who was in the early church in Greece. He was converted at the time that 40 went out from Palestine, and he is closely linked with the Greek Orthodox church that exists today and, through them, with the Russian Orthodox church. When he mentally places himself anywhere to meditate, he sits in a shrine with that round, onion bulb-looking top they put on their churches.

"When we gather information, we bring it back almost as if it were measured by a machine. There are different blocks of color brought back which represent the results obtained, almost like colored mercury enclosed in a barometer. There are scalings at the side, indicating certain intensities and results. Some might indicate lack of concentration, or some a great amount of healing power in a service. From one service which was reported today, we learned that the poor man who was leading the prayers was so concerned about the illness of his wife that a tremendous amount of the healing color was shown in the emanations of that service.

"I am told that I can't tell you the specifics on the various denominations as yet. This is to be a long-term project. However, I can tell you that we are studying the healing impact that is there and the emotional effect of the music, the speech, and the prayers that are there. We are also trying to determine whether the greatest sense of wholeness and unity in worship is achieved in a church that is plain and lacking stained-glass windows, murals, candles, incense, and altars, or whether there is more in those churches which have these artifacts: Is one more mystical than the other?

"These things will not be measured only on Sunday but whenever there are services and gatherings of people. So a portion of each of my days will be spent with this group that is conducting the study."

20
The Universality of Truth

> In my Father's house are many rooms; if it were not so, would I have told you that I go to prepare a place for you? (John 14:2)

During a sitting in March 1971, AD stated, "I am now beginning to feel with every breath, with every thought, and through every pore of the skin, the universality of all truth. It is not until we are away from the density of the physical body that we can be deeply aware of this.

"When I came here, I sought and found the heaven that I knew as a Christian, and as a reader of the truth of the Bible. My faith had brought me to the point where I could understand and appreciate the orientation of the light of Christ. When I am raised toward the light now, it is like a profound ecstasy, a mystical experience, and until you have experienced it and have been caught up without the ties and the cord that keep you in a physical body, it is very difficult to explain.

"You have heard some people say that they feel it doesn't make any difference whether Jesus was or was not. When they do this, they are placing themselves in a trap. They will say, 'I have faith in God and I don't need any intermediaries.' Fine. Perhaps they don't need any saints, but how can they cut out the light of the world—Jesus, the Christ? How *can* they? If they cut out the light of the world, they are dwelling in darkness. On earth when I heard them say, 'I can go straight to God. *I* don't need any intermediaries,' I said, 'Of course you can go straight to God, but do you know *how* to go straight to God? Don't you need a signpost to direct you? Do you have the faith that you can go to God direct?' When I asked them such questions, they became confused. They said, 'Well, through prayer.' And I said, 'Yes, but Jesus taught us how to pray.'[29] They said, 'Well, through faith.' And I responded, 'He taught us what living faith is.' *Jesus reveals the way, the truth, and the life.*

"However, unless we can give someone the true Christian experience of the Christ, it is not *right* for us to say to them, 'You must not be a Buddhist—you must be a Christian.' Unless we can give the true Christian experience of the Christ, then it is far better for us to leave them with the Buddha and that approach to God and to the word. It is wrong for us to say to a Hindu, 'Oh, no, all that is wrong. You must be a Christian.' Unless we can give that man a true and deep understanding of the *meaning* behind the words that Jesus said—the sense of the knowing of the *power* of the meaning behind the word—then we have no *right* to take away their faith because there is an old saying that nature abhors a vacuum.

"I talked the other day with a man who is an ardent Buddhist—a very famous, and very sincere, and very gentle man. His feeling of the Buddha was a much deeper and less turbulent feeling that I have of the Lord Jesus. The turbulence in him is stilled. My guardian and guide said that if I could have looked at my body when I had my first illumination of the

---

[29]In his book *Christian Ethics,* p. 207, AD stated, "The love of the Christian to God constitutes a childlike relationship. This is something new and unique, which Jesus brought into the world. Paul expresses it beautifully when he says that the Christian has received 'the spirit of adoption, whereby we cry, Abba, Father.' (Rom. 8:15) Through Christ the Christian has been taught to regard God as 'Father.' "

Lord Jesus, and I could have looked at the Buddhist's body when he looked at his aspect of God through the Buddha, I would have seen that the Buddhist's body was layered but that mine was smoothly moving. The Buddhist's was in layers, one above the other, but mine was like a cone reaching upward. We Christians meditate and pray, and we think *upward*. We think through our foreheads—we reach *up*. But the Buddhist doesn't. He sits, and it is *here* in the depths of his being."

On March 6, 1971, AD told us there soon would be an opportunity for him to visit a conference. He said, "The conference will take place with a group of incarnate people and a group of the discarnate, and it will take place on the astral plane. They will be there in their astral bodies and will therefore be communicating not so much by thought but by speech. There will be Russians, Chinese, Spanish, English, Americans, and some Hindus at this conference. It has to do with unity. It will deal with the desire to speak of God and to find *one* word that can be used by all peoples and all nations to signify the one God of love—the God of all aspects, and of all faiths and of all religions. There have been a number of conferences and discussions on this taking place over the last fifteen years. To my great pleasure, I was told, when I was taken to one of these conferences in my astral body by my guardian and guide, that I was greeted as an old friend because, while still on earth, I had already been there on three previous occasions in my sleep state. The last time was just prior to the illness that finished my physical body. I found to my amazement that much of the information they spoke about was registered within me, and *I knew it*. This sense of knowing is tremendous. This is the sensing of the future. It is not vision, not clairvoyance, but knowing. And this is the reason that meditation is now becoming so rampant."

On another occasion AD commented further regarding the universality of truth. He stated, "I am still utterly amazed at what I find here. Utterly amazed! There is love and there is harmony. There is music that transcends all thought. There is color, light, belonging, and there is being. It isn't only in the one path of Christianity. You find it in many, many other faiths. All faiths which stress love have this focus. It is like reaching out to a sun and light comes down along different rays.

"We are all walking. We Christians walk here, the Hindus walk there, the Buddhists walk in another place, and so forth. All have their own paradise, goals, aims, and objectives for so long. Then suddenly they are into the tremendous experience of knowing that all is one under God and that there is no division in purpose.

"Since I have been out of the body, it has been my great fortune to have this communion—this attunement and 'at-one-ment' with souls and minds that have been treading a different way, having different beliefs and different conceptions. It is a tremendous, knowing revelation and a great joy to have this understanding, warmth, and at-one-ment. There is one God of us all."

21
Mystical Experiences of Expanding Consciousness

> When all things began, the Word already was. The Word dwelt with God, and what God was, the Word was. . . . All that came to be was alive with his life, and that life was the light of men. The light shines on in the dark, and the darkness has never quenched it. (John 1:1-5)

AD spoke to us about some deeply mystical experiences he had in the realm beyond, stating, "The Holy Spirit may manifest through unseen ones here, and through your own selves directly, but it is always the same source which is manifested and which unifies all things in the created universe. *The Holy Spirit—the creator—is the source of all being.* I had a deep faith in this when I was on earth, but I have now been given experiences which have enabled me to know this truth within the depths of my being, and this is a tremendous fulfillment.

"Through these experiences of expanding consciousness I have changed and am changing. However, this changing is not making me feel more separated from the world and the people I left behind. Instead, it is making me feel closer to you—as if the web of my being is becoming intermingled and weaving in with the web of the beings of all of you. I have a feeling of closer affinity with all people and with all things."

Outer Space

"I had a tremendous experience that I would like to share with you. I know I can't describe it properly, but I will try to share what happened.

"I was having what we call a rest period here, and I thought to myself, 'Well, now I have learned to travel by swift thought—to wing the spirit—and I can arrive very quickly anywhere on the surface of the globe. I really would like to go out and look into space.'

"As soon as I had put forth this desire, I suddenly was conscious of a figure by my side. This figure was taller than I and it had the shape of a physical body with head, shoulders, arms and legs, but it was made of beautiful, vibrating light. The light was similar to the shades, the colors, and the transparency that you see in a crystal. Some of those who come to help us have the milky-lookingness of a pearl. I understand they are nearer to the earth than those beings that come with the appearance of crystal.

"I knew that this being was going to help me have my desired view of the universe, the cosmos. He held out his right hand and I placed my left hand in his. Immediately I was filled with a sense of lightness and expectancy.

"Suddenly—I don't know how it happened—the two of us were out into the deepest of indigo blue, and yet we could see. When I looked around me, all above and around me, there was the deepness of the night sky. I could see the stars—really not a great deal larger than when I used to see them as AD, looking up into the sky from earth. However, they seemed more alive and they were vibrating out at me. I was conscious of the fact that they were moving and that there was an auric light around them—mixtures of gold, blue, pink, and red light—that seemed to be part of the power that was generating around them.

"Suddenly I was flying on my face, looking down. There below me was the moon, with a very slow-moving, milky kind of mistiness around it. As I looked down, I could also see the earth and it was blue. It was moving and revolving and there were parts that I felt I could distinguish as Africa, the North Pole, and other geographical areas of the earth. Around the earth were not only clouds but also lines of fine light —latitudinal and longitudinal lines of power. They were of varying colors, like miniature neon lights.

"Suddenly I saw a streak of light come and it was absorbed into the earth. I though, 'A shooting star!' No, it was impressed on me, it was not a shooting star, but it was a stream of power coming to the earth from the celestial bodies. These streams of power were coming down from all angles to the earth. There were also streams that were going between star and star and star like a tremendous web. These streams of power had a set pattern like a web of a fishing net, which was all continuous with the power of lights pulsating backward and forward. I felt caught up in all of this to the very depths of my being. I felt myself expanding and expanding until I thought, 'I'm going to burst!'

"The moment I thought, 'I'm going to burst!', I suddenly found myself alone, back where this being had met me, and he had gone.

"Then I became conscious of different sounds of bells ringing and music. I realized that I had been hearing these bells and music while I was out in space. In the midst of this sound I became aware of the fact that at the present time I may see and I may observe, but my consciousness will have to expand further before I may know *how* all of this takes place, and *why*.

"I felt a tremendous surge around me—a pulsation and a beat which was unchanging. I also felt lighter pulses and beats which varied and changed. It was as if I could feel deep down in me the steadiness that is ADeeeeeee—a deep awareness of myself as an individual. But above that were all the other rhythms and all the other pulsations, sounds, and vibrations of all other things in the creation. There was a tremendous harmony of sound. It would be impossible to say that it was a symphony, or that it was a chorale, or that I could translate it into music that would go on a treble or a bass clef—that would be impossible. It was more like the most perfect sound that could come, not from a machine such as a huge organ but rather from a living, moving organism.

"We all have our own notes. We all respond and vibrate to our own notes. If each one of us, individually, is part of the great whole, then you can understand all of these notes being sounded—plus all the notes that come from mother earth and the other planets and the stars. Even the so-called 'dead' planets are still emitting vibrations. When there is regression, there is still life, in the same way that when we vacate a physical body, that body is emitting vibrations while returning to the dust of the earth. Thus, even the so-called dead planets are emitting energy and they are transmitting to the whole.

"It is a tremendous feeling to know that one is part of all of this, and it gives one the most powerful sense of belonging. From this experience I knew that it is this sense of belonging that must be given to the people on earth. They must be made to realize that they belong to the great, expanding, universal soul. They belong to the creator. The great truth that has to come through is that not a single thing in the whole of the created universe is isolated, not even a speck of iron. All things are interconnected through the power and the spirit of the creator, and no one is ever alone."

The Logos and Creation

In a succeeding sitting AD stated, "I had another experience which is also difficult to describe. I was sitting and meditating about the biblical passage in the Gospel of St. John, "In the beginning was the Word, and the Word was with God'' (John 1:1), and I was trying to visualize what it must have been like. The one who is my guide and teacher here was by my side, and he sensed my thought. Suddenly I found myself standing on what must have been an elevation, because down below me were spread out all the parts of the earth at once as if I could see through the earth. I could see the cold spans and the tropical areas. I could see places which one would call gardens of Eden, and others which were barren, wild, and desert. It all seemed to be laid out in front of me.

"Then it disappeared, and all I saw was the most beautiful blending of colors, every color—colors that I never could have thought of—and I felt caught up in them. I was drifting and moving with them. I was conscious of the fact that there was a myriad of sounds around me.

"I suddenly became aware of myself as just a *pinpoint of knowing*. I wasn't rationalizing anything. I was just knowing. I knew that all that sound, and all this color, would settle and become the planet earth as I knew it. I knew also that above me were other colors and vibrations and sounds and music, and that these were going to go out and make other planets and other stars.

"I then remembered the experience of being out in outer space and seeing what I felt was the universe—an experience even more marvelous than that of the astronauts going to the moon. I realized that they only saw the physical and I was really seeing the *essence*. The moment I realized that, there were many, many perfumes. I *knew* that this is the next stage in the evolution of man. Man is going to know by the sense of smell, as well as by sound, by sight, and by knowing.

"This whole experience seemed to continue for a very, very long time. I can't tell you how long, and I can't tell you all of the colors I saw or describe completely what happened. However, the next thing I knew, I was just being held and placed and I heard a voice saying, *'Don't think—just know.'*

And how can I translate into words that I *knew*? It wasn't 'Now we see through a glass darkly, but then face to face'—it was more than that.

"Out of this experience I gained the knowledge that the essence of all is like a thread, and we may see ourselves as beautiful beads on that thread or we can see ourselves as very heavy pieces of lead, noncomprehending, depending on the degree to which we are in tune with the universe and the laws God has laid down. We have to remember that we do not live at the height of ecstasy all the time. There is compensation in the pendulum swing between the negative and the positive. However, *the ultimate goal in the evolution of man is to reach the point where each man, each sacred personality created, is in tune and is, as it were, a beautiful bead on the thread of the essence of the whole.*"

Epilogue from AD

"It seems to me that the best way I can use my abilities now is to travel as much as I can here and to bring through to you the experiences that I see and know, as objectively as I can give them.

"I want to explore my universe—this ever-expanding universe here. I want to expand it. I want to be able to tell you what it's like.

"There is no time when one can say, 'I know it all' or 'that's the end.' Knowledge is ever-unfolding, as are life, time, space, and consciousness."

APPENDIXES

1
Vita, Alvin Daniel Mattson—
1895-1970

Student

AD was a graduate of Augustana College and Theological Seminary at Rock Island, Illinois. He later did graduate work at Yale University Divinity School, where his great concern for social justice was developed as well as his interest in the study of parapsychology. He was a student all his life, constantly studying new developments in many fields. To him knowledge was ever unfolding and he often said, "If anyone gets to the point where he thinks he knows it all, he had better watch out!"

Parish Pastor

His early ministry in the Lutheran Church included rural parishes where he learned to appreciate the men who farm our lands, and where he developed his early ecological concerns for man's proper stewardship of the natural resources God has given us. Ecology was a vital, vocal concern of AD's over forty years ago.

Theological Professor

He served as Professor of Christianity at Upsala College in East Orange, New Jersey, and at Augustana College in Rock Island, Illinois. He later became a professor at Augustana Theological Seminary (now the Lutheran School of Theology, Chicago), where he taught for thirty-six years. At the seminary he was Chairman of the Department of Christian Ethics and Sociology.

Author

His teachings went far beyond his classroom via his writings. Two of his books, *Christian Ethics* and *Christian Social Consciousness*, were widely used as textbooks in seminaries throughout the United States. *Christian Ethics* also was translated into Chinese for use in Far Eastern seminaries.

Labor Chaplain

The oldest son of a Lutheran minister in a family of six children, AD worked on railroad gangs and on factory assembly lines to earn money for his college and seminary education. His lifelong concern for adequate wages and decent working conditions for the laboring man stemmed from his own experience.

For many years he was Protestant Chaplain of the Quad-City Federation of Labor, a delegate body representing 30,000 workers and headquartered at Rock Island, Illinois. He was often called by both management and labor to mediate their differences. In 1950 he was assigned by the U.S. State Department to make a special study of the labor conditions in postwar Germany.

Traveler

Not content to learn about social problems from books, AD traveled widely in this nation and throughout the world to study the plight of the underprivileged. He also conducted travel seminars for his students to give them firsthand experience with various social problems.

2
The "Evidential"

"Evidential" material is that which gives substantiation to the identity of the communicator from beyond. There is strong evidential that AD is the communicator, based on situation verification and the nuances of AD's personality that come through.

After the first group of sittings, intentional evidential material was not given too frequently. AD pointed out in a sitting in February 1972 that he already had given a goodly amount of evidential to assure us of his identity. He stated that he does not intend to deplete his mind-directive power and stored energy by continually giving evidential. Rather, his purpose is to bring through information that will extend our vision and be of value to our living experience here on earth. (On occasion he has stated that his mind-directive "current" was running out and we have had to break for a time, indicating that the energy power with which the invisibles communicate is not unlimited.)

The following sections point up some of the significant

evidential. Some evidential material, of a very personal nature pertaining to the immediate family, is not included.

Life's Disciplines

In the first sitting on March 2, 1971, AD spoke about the disciplines of life: "So many people have the feeling that they must work according to the way *they* feel. They say, 'Lord, use us,' but they don't want to be garbage men or they don't want to be a lot of things which God might want them to be." And humorously he continued, "They might have to cook, even. That, too, is a discipline. When I could accept it as a discipline, and get my juicer going, then I could enjoy even that.

"This is something that has to be taught to people—that the disciplines of life are those that are imposed by the surroundings and the obligations to society. God doesn't impose the disciplines. He gives us perfect freedom in spirit. It is we who have to put our disciplines on ourselves."

The above section contains several very evidential points. When on earth AD constantly stressed the sacredness of human personality and the importance of each person to the total scheme of things. This applied to the various vocations people have, as well. He often would illustrate this to us by pointing out that all honest, contributing labor was essential to the total scheme of things and of equal worth in the sight of God—from the *garbage man* to the *academician*. Therefore, his specific mention that "they don't want to be garbage men" was very significant to me.

The comment about his cooking and his juicer also is very significant, as one of AD's burdens in life, after my mother died, was cooking. He finally got a juicer, which he enjoyed using, and made a very thorough study of nutrition and diet. He would often demonstrate the juicer to people who visited his cabin. (Margaret knew nothing about the juicer or his dislike of cooking.)

An "Original"

Later in the first sitting he said, "Now I don't want you to think of me as a typical minister. I don't want you to think of me as a typical anything, because I was an *original*."

This was said in jest to make us laugh, but anyone who knew AD would agree that this was a good description of him. He always was many years ahead of his time in trying to lead the church out into the world to champion the causes of social justice and reform. His Commission on Morals and Social Problems of the Augustana Church, which he chaired for more than twenty-six years, was often the first among Protestant church commissions to come forth with resolutions against racism and war and to deal with such problems as birth control and the population explosion.

When Karl Barth's theology, stressing that God is "wholly other," was at its peak AD could not accept it. Instead, he went against the trend of the day and stressed the dynamic reality of the Kingdom of God. He recognized God as living and active, accomplishing his purposes in the realm of human history. AD saw this as a permanent dynamic for all time. He wrote:

> God is not geographically transcendent, in any faraway manner, on some celestial throne, waiting to be discovered by man. He is living and active and makes Himself known through His activity as He rules in His Kingdom. When this is recognized, theology becomes dynamic rather than static. It will then no longer be merely a matter of conserving and perpetuating doctrines, but it will concern itself with the resistance which is to be overcome and the great ends which are to be gained.[30]

[30] A. D. Mattson, *Christian Social Consciousness* (Rock Island, Ill.: Augustana Book Concern, 1953), pp. 106-107.

Dahlias

In the Section on "The Process of Communication," p. 13, AD describes what my aura looks like to him. He says, "The rose pink comes out like big flower petals, like big spiky dahlia petals."

This did not strike me as evidential until I was transcribing the tapes, when I realized the significance of the specific mention of *dahlia* petals. Although AD appreciated most flowers, dahlias were his favorites and at one time he grew many varieties of them with great success. When visiting us in New York, he enjoyed visiting the Botanical Gardens to view the dahlia beds.

Orange-colored Chairs

On several occasions during communications Margaret received "pictures" and remarked, "They are sitting on orange-colored chairs, comfortable-looking *orange-colored* chairs."

With so much material coming through, I also didn't "register" this evidential until I was replaying some of the tapes when the manuscript was almost complete. The orange-colored chairs are very evidential. If AD was going to have a chair in the astral world, it would certainly be orange-colored as that was one of his favorite colors. At his cabin in Minnesota I had been requested to make orange-colored drapes for the whole cabin. There he also chose orange-colored chairs, kitchen bar stools, table, lamps, and dressers.

Whole-Hearted Commitment to God

In chap. 2, p. 32, AD states, "There are very few who will throw themselves into the sea of the Holy Spirit. Some merely put their toe in and tentatively feel it. The years of putting toes in are past, and the time has come to throw yourself in."

This, again, is very typically AD. Tentative, halfway measures on the part of people in their relation to God and his Kingdom were always a source of pain to AD. He constantly urged a wholehearted and courageous witness for God and his purposes in the world.

AD's Father

In the first sitting AD mentioned contacts with certain relatives who were dead but did not mention his father. In the second sitting I asked if he had seen his father.

AD said, "Strangely enough, yes, because I hadn't appreciated I would need the help that my father could give me when I passed over. I hadn't appreciated how important it would be to me. I had rather thought that I would need the help of my mother, of my wife, and maybe of my brother. But somehow or other my father's impression on earth had formed me in a certain way and I didn't feel that this certain way would need to be picked up anymore. But Father has been extremely helpful to me in adjusting to the conditions of this new life. . . . He is a dear soul and has made a great deal of progress and really is way beyond me at the moment."

When they were both on earth, the views of AD and his father differed greatly and were sometimes a source of contention. AD's father was a Lutheran minister with a rather pietistic approach to religion and life, and he had been a stern disciplinarian in enforcing his pietistic beliefs. But AD was nonpietistic, very undogmatic, and open in his outlook on life. Therefore, AD's statement that he hadn't appreciated he would need the help of his father when he passed over, is very evidential.

The Amos Notes

AD mentioned that he had never finished a series of talks and lessons on the Bible that he had been giving. He said that I should surely have found some notes that he had ready to use and that I had his full permission to use them anytime I liked: They were there to be used.

I did find these notes in a zippered leather envelope at his cabin. They were on the Book of Amos. He had been conducting a study on the Book of Amos for a group of people who lived around the Minnesota lake where his cabin was located.

Don't Weep

During the second sitting, when AD was describing the experience of his death to Margaret and me, I couldn't help crying. He said to me, "Don't cry, Ruth. You didn't cry then. What are you crying for now?"

This was very significant and evidential to me.

My brother Al and I had been at AD's bedside when he died. Al and I had stood on either side of his bed, holding his arms as he was going out. I had made up my mind that I would not cry as I wanted him to be released without any sense of being held back by tears I might shed. (Margaret did not know that I had not wept when I witnessed his death.)

Favorite Flannel Shirt

In the third session Margaret was given a "picture" of AD's reception by his family and friends when he passed over. After a description of some of the people who met him, Margaret said to me, "They seem to be wearing ordinary clothes —shirts, short-sleeved shirts, white knit shirts, trousers. They don't seem to be dressed in *robes*. Your father, as well, is dressed in gray trousers and he has a checked shirt on." AD had a checked, flannel shirt that he always enjoyed wearing, so I immediately asked, "His favorite checked flannel shirt?" Margaret said it was.

Margaret then took time out to tell me that her sister, after she was dead, always appeared to clairvoyants in a favorite checked suit that she had enjoyed wearing when she was on earth.

AD then said to us, "That is perfectly right. You see, you have to think yourself into clothes over here. Your sister found it easier always to appear in her checked suit, which everyone recognized. So it was with me. When I was on earth, I didn't even think about clothes. I'd get up in the morning and I'd put on the first thing that was handy. Well, I stepped out of the physical body at the hospital and picked up the first clothes that were handy."

I didn't know what AD had worn to the hospital when he became ill. My brother Al had taken AD to the hospital, and Al later told me that AD had worn gray trousers and the favorite checked flannel shirt to the hospital. Al and I both felt that this was certainly good evidential.

Inner Dynamo

In the second group of sittings AD said, "When I was on earth, there was always with me a sense of urgency. I frequently felt, when I was going around among people, that there was a dynamo going inside of me that said, 'You haven't got much time. You must do this. You must do that." I would sit back in my chair and try to relax, and I would look at people who seemed to be going along rather quietly, and I would wonder, 'Why should I have this feeling?'

"I had always imagined, as a younger man, that when I got toward 'old age' I would be quite content to sit back and browse in my thinking and watch the world go by. Somehow it didn't happen that way. In the days when I was a young man, I was chasing around the countryside or racing through books. Now in my 'old age' I was getting just as much activity going in my mind, in the narrow confines of where I was, as in the days when I traveled hundreds of miles. I realized that this pushing and driving was the accumulation of the things that needed to be done—pushing, pushing toward me. It made me feel as if there was this whirring dynamo inside me, which gave me energy."

Anyone who knew AD will testify to the dynamic movement in his life up to the very end. The sermon preached at AD's funeral illustrates this evidential:

> "If only in this life . . ." says Paul. There was a tentativeness about life (says Paul), an uncertainty. This AD understood. There was something incomplete about life. But the now was significant. AD relished life. He savored its goodness. Each day spelled opportunity for him. He did not bask in the light of prior accomplishments but sought new avenues of service in his retirement years. "This is the day that the Lord has made. Let us rejoice and be glad in it." This he believed and lived. He did not settle into a comfortable niche. In his life there was movement.
> When you confronted AD and you sought to nail him down so you'd be quite sure that when you returned you'd find him there, you'd be doomed to disappointment. The now was not something simply to be accepted but to be acted upon.[31]

Constant Johnson

On February 28, 1972, we had a very objective evidential incident. Before a sitting on that day Margaret said to me, "Who is Constant Johnson? Your father tells me that he has not been well and that he will soon be over with them." The Reverend Dr. Constant Johnson was a classmate of AD from

---

[31] From the funeral sermon preached by the Reverend Allen C. Nelson at St. John's Lutheran Church, Rock Island, Illinois. October 23, 1970.

seminary days and a well-known clergyman in the Augustana Lutheran Church. I had known him when I was a small girl but certainly had not thought about him in many years, nor had I had any contact with him or his family. I certainly knew nothing about his health, or even if he were alive or dead. I decided to watch the obituary notices in *The Lutheran,* and in the April 19, 1972 issue of this magazine I found a notice of Dr. Constant Johnson's death, which occurred on March 14, 1972.

3
Man's Responsibility in Achieving Harmony in God's Kingdom: Quotes from AD's Writings

In his book *The Social Responsibility of Christians,* AD had some significant things to say about man's responsibility in achieving harmony in God's Kingdom:

"It is God who exercises his sovereignty and, therefore, his kingdom is . . . 'given.' The sovereignty of God does not depend upon man's will or activity. At no place in the New Testament are we told to 'build the kingdom.' It is already established 'from the foundations of the world.' . . . We can 'see . . . enter . . . proclaim' and 'suffer' for it. But we cannot build it. The kingdom is something to be accepted, submitted to and obeyed. The rulers of this world have their day, but the ultimate authority is God's. . . .

"Then what of human responsibility? Neither activism nor quietism is an answer to our question. The Christian will not become passive to responsibilities in the social order and simply wait for a celestial relief expedition. There are types of modern theology which leave the impression that the theologian is interested in the doctrine of creation and in the doctrine of the parousia, but expects nothing to happen between those poles. This attitude involves the thought that despair and defeatism are the only realistic attitudes with respect to the whole realm of history. . . .

"The Christian does have a responsibility for the character of society because he has been laid hold of by the powers of the kingdom, and those powers work in and through him. Paul realized it was God who was bringing in his kingdom, but that fact did not release Paul from a tremendous missionary task. Paul could say, 'It is God who worketh in you both to will and to work,' but he could also speak of his 'labor' for the Lord (Phil. 2:13,16). The prophets of the Old Testament often spoke of the exodus from Egypt as the work of God (Amos 9:7), but Moses was given a task to perform in connection with that deliverance. God performed his deliverance through the instrumentality of a man. A secular historian might write an account of the exodus from the point of view of the leadership afforded by Moses, but the sacred historian sees, back of the human instrumentality, the movements of God in history. . . .

"The kingdom is a gift, but the powers of the kingdom operate through human agents. The kingdom is the supreme gift of God, but by virtue of this, it also becomes for each of us, our supreme task. God establishes his kingdom, but in so doing he takes us into his service. Man's activity in the interest of the kingdom of God is God's activity in man. To wait for the coming of the kingdom in the spirit of quietism is not true to the genius and the dynamic power of the Christian faith. A gift is bestowed upon us, but that gift involves a call to a task in which God uses men as his instruments. This task is more than an effort to help men understand themselves and God's will for them as individuals. It involves the whole realm of history and society, and the transformation of human institutions for human betterment."[32]

[32] A. D. Mattson, *The Social Responsibility of Christians* (Philadelphia: Muhlenberg Press, 1960), pp. 52-54. Used by special permission of the Board of Publication of the Lutheran Church in America, and the Knubel-Miller Foundation Lectures.

4
Quotes from Hymns and Prayers of Christendom

It is interesting to note that many of the hymns and prayers of Christendom, contained in the hymn and prayer book that AD used, reflect the believers' assurance, which was AD's assurance, of union with God and the Communion of Saints in the present life. They reflect also the conviction, which was AD's conviction, that through union with God the believer even now experiences communion with the faithful departed. Christians who have sung these hymns and prayed these prayers may now find new meaning in them.[33]

(The Church) on earth hath union
With God, the Three in One,
And mystic sweet communion
With those whose rest is won. (Hymn 149:4)

---

[33]These hymns and prayers can be traced to many different backgrounds. They are quoted from the *Service Book and Hymnal* of the Lutheran Church in America (copyright 1958) with special permission of the Board of Publication of the Lutheran Church in America.

O, Almighty God, who has knit together thine
elect in one communion and fellowship in the
mystical body of thy Son, Christ our Lord ...
(Prayer, p. 114)

... we remember before thee, O everlasting God, all our
friends and kindred who have passed within the veil. Keep us
in union with them here, through faith and love towards thee.
(Prayer, p. 224)

O blest communion, fellowship divine ...
All are one in thee, for all are thine. (Hymn 144:4)

Adoring praises now we bring
And with the heavenly blessed sing. (Hymn 103:4)

Before us and beside us
Still holden in thine hand,
A cloud unseen of witness
Our elder comrades stand:
One family unbroken,
We join, with one acclaim,
One heart, one voice uplifting,
To glorify thy Name. (Hymn 248:4)

We remember with thanksgiving those who have loved
and served thee in thy Church on earth. . . . Keep us in
fellowship with all thy saints. (Prayer, p. 8)

O God, who hast brought us near to an innumerable company
of angels, and to the spirits of just men
made perfect: Grant us during our earthly pilgrimage
to abide in their fellowship. (Prayer, p. 224)

Through Jesus Christ our Lord, who in the blessedness of
thy saints hath given us a glorious pledge of the hope of our
calling: that, following their example and
being strengthened by their fellowship, we may exult in
thee for thy mercy, even as they rejoice with thee
in glory. Therefore with Angels and Archangels, and
with all the company of heaven, we laud and magnify thy
glorious name. (Prayer, p. 10-11)

Join we with the heavenly host,
Singing everlastingly
To the blessed Trinity. (Hymn 135:4)

Almighty God, who by the death of thy Son, Jesus
Christ, has destroyed death . . . and by his glorious
resurrection has brought life and immortality to
light . . . keep us, who are still in the body, in
everlasting fellowship with all that wait for thee
on earth, and with all around thee in heaven, in
union with him who is the Resurrection and the Life,
even Jesus Christ our Lord. Amen. (Prayer, p. 269)

5 Bibliography for Suggested Reading

This bibliography is suggested for the reader who is not yet familiar with the paranormal area. It lists but a sample of the various books and journals relating to this field.

Books

Bach, Marcus. *The Power of Perception.* New York: Hawthorn, 1973.

Cayce, Hugh Lynn. *Venture Inward.* New York: Harper & Row, 1964.

Chardin, Pierre Teilhard de. *The Phenomenon of Man.* Trans. by Bernard Wall. New York: Harper & Row, 1959.

Crookall, Robert, D. *The Supreme Adventure: Analyses of Psychic Communications.* London: James Clarke, 1961.

Eddy, Sherwood. *You Will Survive after Death.* Highland Park, Ill.: Clark Publishing, 1950.

Greber, Johannes. *Communication with the Spirit World of God.* Teaneck, N.J.: Johannes Greber Memorial

Foundation (139 Hillside Ave.; Teaneck, N.J. 07666), 1958.

Harlowe, S. Ralph. *A Life After Death.* New York: Macfadden-Bartell, 1961.

James, William. *The Varieties of Religious Experience.* New York: Macmillan, 1961.

Inge, W. R. *Christian Mysticism.* New York: Meridian Books, 1956.

Johnson, Kendall. *The Living Aura.* New York: Hawthorn, 1975.

Kilner, Walter J. *The Human Aura.* New Hyde Park, N.Y.: University Books, 1965.

Leadbeater, C. W. *The Chakras.* Wheaton, Ill.: Theosophical Publishing House, 1966.

LeShan, Lawrence. *The Medium, the Mystic and the Clairvoyant, Towards a General Theory of the Paranormal.* New York: Viking, 1974.

Murphy, Gardner. *Challenge of Psychical Research: A Primer of Parapsychology.* World Perspective Series, planned and edited by Ruth Nanda Anshen, vol. 26, New York: Harper & Row, 1961.

Osis, Karlis. *Deathbed Observations by Physicians and Nurses.* New York: Parapsychology Foundation, 1961.

Ostrander, Sheila, and Schroeder, Lynn. *Psychic Discoveries Behind the Iron Curtain.* Englewood Cliffs, N.J.: Prentice-Hall, 1971.

Pike, James, A. *The Other Side.* New York: Dell, 1968.

Rauscher, William V., with Allen Spraggett. *The Spiritual Frontier.* Garden City, N.Y.: Doubleday, 1975.

Rhine, J. B. *New World of the Mind.* New York: William Sloane Associates, 1953.

Smith, Susy. *ESP.* New York: Pyramid Publications, 1962.

Sugrue, Thomas. *There Is a River: The Story of Edgar Cayce.* New York: Dell, 1970.

Underhill, Evelyn. *Mysticism.* New York: E. P. Dutton, 1961.

Vaughan, Alan. *Patterns of Prophecy.* New York: Hawthorn, 1973.
Walker, Jeanne. *Always, Karen.* New York: Hawthorn, 1975.
Weatherhead, Leslie. *Life Begins at Death.* New York: Abingdon, 1970.
White, Stewart Edward. *The Betty Book.* New York: E. P. Dutton, 1937.
_____. *The Unobstructed Universe.* New York: E. P. Dutton, 1959.

Journals

The ARE Journal. Published by the Association for Research and Enlightenment, Virginia Beach, Va.

Journal of the American Society for Psychical Research. Published by the American Society for Psychical Research, Inc., New York, N.Y.

Journal of Parapsychology. Published by the Parapsychology Press of the Foundation for Research on the Nature of Man, Durham, N.C.

Parapsychology Review. Published by the Parapsychology Foundation, Inc., New York, N.Y.

Spiritual Frontiers. Published by the Spiritual Frontiers Fellowship, Inc., Evanston, Ill.

Theta. Published by the Psychical Research Foundation, Inc., Durham, N.C.